The Charisma Within

The Charisma Within

15 STEPS TO ENHANCE YOUR INNER MAGNETISM

Happy Ali

HAPPY INSIGHTS

HAPPY INSIGHTS

Copyright © 2021 Happy Insights

All rights reserved.

No part of this book may be reproduced by any means without express written permission of the publisher.

ISBN: 978-0-578-34012-8

www.happyinsights.net

This book is dedicated to anyone who has been plagued by insecurities.

CONTENTS

Acknowledgments..i

Introduction...1

The Beginning...11

Step One: Make Peace With Where You Are In Your Life..27

Step Two: Make Peace With Your Body...................39

Step Three: Detach From Praise And Criticism..........55

Step Four: Know Your Inherent Value...................69

Step Five: Never Try to Impress Anyone with More Than You Are..81

Step Six: Be Picky Choosing Your Friends..............93

Step Seven: Make A Decision to Release the Guards That Hide Your Flaws...105

Step Eight: Put Happiness On Top Of Your Priority List..117

Step Nine: Do Not Categorize Yourself................137

Step Ten: Know That Everyone of Us Is Worthy Of Everything We Desire.....................................151

Step Eleven: Be Emotionally Self-Sufficient..........161

Step Twelve: Make A Daily Statement to Yourself to Be Reminded of Your Worthiness.............................171

Step Thirteen: Decide Never To Lie to Make Yourself Look Better Than You Are......................................181

Step Fourteen: Don't Judge People from A Single Aspect of Their Personality **189**

Step Fifteen: Take Responsibility for The Energy Your Add to A Room, Interaction, Or Conversation..................**199**

Conclusion......................…..…………………....**207**

Acknowledgements

I would like to thank everyone who believed in me and encouraged me to pursue my path of helping others. Without the support of my mother, all my best friends (Rain, Alexis, Alfonso, Jason, Tricia, and Guy, just to name a few), and the rest of my family (father, sisters, nieces, aunts, uncles, cousins, and my grandmother), this book would not be possible. Thank you to my children, Faith, Sky, Dario, and Syrus, for inspiring me to be a better person. A GIANT thank you to Rachel and Jordan for being my best friends and the best co-parents that I could ever ask for. Thank you to Skye Byrne, Lisa Kaas Boyle, and Jeremy Lane for spending the time to go through this book in different stages and give me advice. I would also like to thank Esther Hicks for all her continuous inspiration. Finally, I would like to thank Rhonda Byrne for opening the rabbit hole that led me to the events that made this book happen.

"Charisma is a sparkle in people that money can't buy. It's an invisible energy with visible effects."

MARIANNE WILLIAMSON

Introduction

When I began writing this book, I only had one intention and that was to write a book that could help anyone who reads it manage their life and their relationships with themselves and others. I strongly believe that most people inherently know what to do to live a great life, but I also believe that sometimes people get caught up in the moment and forget. That is why I am here to remind you, in case you forgot! Now, let's start with these simple questions!

- What if we all thought the same thoughts?
- How would the world be if we all looked the same?
- What if we all enjoyed the same things?

- What if there was only one type of food to eat?
- Would life be interesting?
- Would there be growth?
- Would there be excitement?

Probably not, and if so, to a much smaller degree. The good news is that there is more than one kind of food to eat. We all like a variety of things. People's thoughts are formed from unique perspectives. And we are not all the same.

There is so much variety in this world that anyone can find someone who likes the things they do and appreciates the way they think. All it takes is a bit of courage to allow the real you to surface without trying to mold it into something that takes away from your most authentic self. If who you really are is fully displayed, then those who appreciate you can find you with greater ease. Unfortunately, in an attempt to gain friends and status, people misrepresent themselves and try to become someone they are not. We lie all the

INTRODUCTION

time! We lie not only with our words but also how we present ourselves. We now have photo enhancing filters at our disposal and many images we see of others are greatly edited and curated. Yet still, you would be surprised to know that in most cases, even in that misrepresentation, deceit is not a factor. It is the simple desire to belong, to feel acceptance, and to be loved. It's about nothing more than insecurities. Though many of us gain a certain amount of love and acceptance for the facade we display, the absence of inner love and respect becomes more and more apparent and begins to take its toll, not just on our own psyche but also in the quality of the people we attract to our lives. In an attempt to fit in, people hide qualities within themselves that another would adore. When you do not love yourself, you are not at your best and those you interact with tend to be very similar. Call it karma or whatever you wish, but this seems to be the cycle that many people fall into. You must stop to consider what people are mostly attracted to. What is it about certain people that appeals to just about anyone they come in contact with? Though a lot of people would state that you could never truly pinpoint what that is, I can tell you that it is not that difficult either. It is a simple magnetic field that starts inside of us and surrounds us charged with love, balance, appreciation, and an authentic expression of self. It is through those means that you can build your confidence and exude charisma.

There is nothing more attractive than someone who is so confident that they radiate divine energy. An energy that is a life-giving force that attracts in a powerful yet effortless way. Those who love themselves seem to be loved by the most people. But it all starts with your own mind, and the way you think. Being attractive is usually misinterpreted into the possession of beauty, money, or status. Though these things do seem to attract others, they can also fuel insecurities. It is not a secret that impressive looks, fame, or status can attract a stranger, but these qualities are not substantial enough to sustain great relationships. Don't get me

INTRODUCTION

wrong, there is nothing wrong with physical beauty, fame, or financial abundance, but when used solely as a way of measuring self-worth, these qualities can leave a person with a great fear of loss. The happiness of the individual will become unstable and dependent upon how long they can maintain their status and beauty.

Fortunately, our true ability to attract has very little to do with money, fame, or beauty. I know that some would disagree, but there are many individuals who have come to this conclusion on their own. As I mentioned earlier, it is important to know that within each person exists a magnetic quality that exceeds any physical attribute. Those who have mastered or witnessed this magnetic quality have often referred to it as charisma. No matter what you call it, some have learned how to enhance their own magnetic quality. Though some seem to have it more than others, there is not one person alive who cannot nurture and master their inner magnet to its fullest potential. It is every human being's birthright to shine as bright as possible.

THE CHARISMA WITHIN

We are all meant to be shining stars lighting up the universe. Our inner magnet is how we shine and how we attract others, and the strength of our magnet is dependent upon our consciousness and what ideas are currently active in our minds. Our magnetism is contingent on the beliefs we have about ourselves and our place in this world. Even when we think we are attracting people because of beauty or success, it is neither the beauty nor the success that attracts but instead the underlying confidence that enhances the attraction. Most people give all the credit to external qualities, but that only makes their magnetic quality dependent on having the things that they have given credit to. That is why it is important to know how to enhance one's own magnetic quality with little or no external help. Though it is quite possible to enhance your superficial attractive qualities using external help, once you pass a certain stage of personal development, further growth will depend solely on your ability to look within and allow the most authentic version of you to shine.

INTRODUCTION

I am sure there are a lot of people who wish they were just a little prettier, a little taller, had more money, were born into a different family, or were just born as someone else so they would be more loved, appreciated, or simply noticed. This book is not only for those people but anyone who wants to milk every ounce of their own personality, not only for their own benefit but also for the world's. In this book, I will show you how I think it is that we exude true charisma. I will explain what it is that people are drawn to and how anyone can go about achieving it. I do have to be honest; this is not a book that will simply transform your life just because you have read it. Unless you apply what you learn one step at a time, this book can be nothing but an interesting read. I must admit that at first it takes some effort (more for some than others), and it might feel like an impossible task, but like learning any new skill, practice is imperative. And with a little time and patience, these steps will become second nature. So much that to return to your previous patterns of thought will take more effort than sustaining your newly found wisdom and way of being. Fortunately, there are many steps to enhancing your inner magnet, so if one seems to be difficult, you can learn about that step quickly, put it to the side, and work on ones that seem easier in your current state of being. Though, once you begin to see results, you will be motivated to take further action, and will want to master all the steps as soon as possible. That being said, I have placed each step in a very specific order for maximum efficacy.

But before we go any further, let's review some of the concepts I covered in the previous section.

1. Most people want to feel loved and accepted.
2. People will go out of their way to feel attractive—mostly focusing on external qualities as their source of attraction.
3. Relying on external qualities can leave you in fear of losing your confidence.

INTRODUCTION

4. There is an invisible magnetic field that surrounds us and is the true source of our attraction.
5. You can see evidence of that magnetic field at work when you meet charismatic people that do not possess traditional beauty, wealth, or status.
6. Anyone can enhance his or her own magnetic field to its fullest potential.
7. The way to enhance your magnetic field is through your thoughts and beliefs about self.
8. If you learn to enhance your magnet from within, you can never be in fear of losing your confidence.

There are simple steps that can dramatically enhance your magnetic field with sufficient practice.

If you can find yourself in little or no opposition to the statements above, you can easily benefit from the steps that follow. However, if you feel any disconnection to my words, the following steps might

THE CHARISMA WITHIN

not reap you much benefit. There are as many types of ways to improve our lives as there are people who inhabit this earth, and though one process might work substantially for some, it cannot work for everyone. The only way to know if a concept is valuable to you is to see how you feel when you are learning about it. Your feelings will always let you know if something is of value to you or not. The only reason that I chose to include this paragraph is that I wanted only those who felt comfortable with the idea of having an inner magnet to read on and explore.

The Beginning

Growing up, I remember how much I disliked the constant emphasis placed on people's outward appearance. Looking flawless was my family's mantra. In truth, this type of thinking was not exclusive to my family but ingrained in my culture. It was a way of life that we were taught as young children. Yet, I couldn't help but grow tired of seeing people's value assessed based primarily upon their looks, status, and fortune. Even worse, most people I was raised with felt only as valuable as others thought them to be. I was told that you had to maintain a nearly perfect outer image regardless of what was happening on the inside.

THE CHARISMA WITHIN

Keeping up the infallible facade was vital, even if you were crumbling on the inside. I remember being constantly reminded that if other people thought I was successful, I was in fact successful. I was told that I needed to blend in with society, and the only exception to the rule was in the case of great achievements and accolades. Only then was I able to not only showcase my uniqueness but also wear it as a badge of honor. That type of thinking never resonated with me and instead gave birth to a great rebellion inside, and even though I had been a relatively "compliant" child, something new was stirring up inside of me. All I wanted to do was to leave my old-fashioned family and live beyond those false ideals. I was terrified and insecure, but I had grown tired of seeing people portraying false images of themselves in an attempt to be accepted and loved. I believed my family was wrong and hoped that the rest of the world would know better.

Despite my fears and lack of confidence, I moved

THE BEGINNING

out of my parents' house at the age of sixteen, and, for a moment, I felt some relief. I began to meet quite authentic people, and I must say that even the people I saw on the big screen seemed to be unique and different. In the early nineties, individuality was being celebrated, and that concept was a breath of fresh air. Well. . . that was 1994, and now we are starting the third decade of the new millennium.

Unfortunately, the joyous days of celebrated individuality were short-lived. Twenty-seven years later, I look around to see the harmful effects that Hollywood norms and social media standards have had on society, not just in the United States but also all around the globe, and it seems that the emphasis on beauty, status, and fame are greatly amplified. My family is now tame compared to what the world has become. The obsession with looking good has taken a life of its own. A large percentage of people on most media platforms have begun to look the same. Women are becoming apparent clones, sharing very similar physical characteristics carefully crafted not just by doctors and digital filters but also with the use of photoshop and extreme makeup contouring. Minus the passing "Dad Bod" phase, most men have (or want) six-pack abs to look more like Ken Dolls than actual human beings. People of all ages pose in front of backdrops that make their lives appear richer than reality. I eventually had to conclude that it was not just my family trying to feel accepted, it was the entire world. However, now on a much larger and much more generic scale. The scary part is that this era is just beginning. If left unchecked, who knows what the world will become in the future.

Nowadays, there are more people trying to fit in with the crowds than ever. People are dimming their individual lights and replacing them with generic reflections of the false images created by the media. Beauty has become standardized and that is not great news. More and more people are lying about themselves to fit the socially accepted mold. It takes a

THE BEGINNING

small taste of positive feedback on social media to get anyone to crave more attention and approval. All anyone has to do is compare the number of likes a carefully posed and edited thirst trap photo will receive compared to a photo showing something deeply profound and meaningful. The problem is that attention is not only addictive but also fleeting.

Personally, I have fallen into these traps on more occasions than I would like to admit, and every time I crawl out, I fall right back in only to crawl my way back out again. So even I, a person creating this material to help others, am an example of what is happening to the global psyche. Luckily, I feel that I have enough inner love and support to be able to shift my own personal balance to prevent the extreme grip of the irresistible traps. Self-confidence is alarmingly fading, but luckily reversible. I have faith in the reversal because I have experienced the benefit of genuine self-confidence that stems from within and not without. I know that I would not have the ability to crawl out of these traps if I was not lucky enough to learn some important and challenging lessons in my adolescence.

In 1988, my family moved from Iran to the United States. I was a ten-year-old that did not speak English, had two giant front teeth, and possessed noticeable effeminate characteristics. I was unfamiliar with American culture and ungifted at all the new sports that I had never seen or heard about. I grew up during the Iran and Iraq War, and our television was restricted to the content allowed by the newly formed Islamic Republic of Iran. The Western world was demonized, and even music was outlawed. Of course, we listened to bootleg music, but it was forbidden and cause for arrest. The only thing that was still legal was soccer, but even in that sport, I was terrible. I couldn't kick a ball to save my life. Now, in my new home in Los Angeles, I had to learn to play sports such as baseball, basketball, and football. In baseball, I had to use a bat while praying to hit the tiny white ball that always failed to make contact. In football, I had to catch elongated balls

THE BEGINNING

flying at my face, despite my horrible hand-eye coordination. My short stature didn't help me much either. I won't even go into basketball; I am sure you can use your imagination to know how I fared compared to the exceptionally tall and skilled players.

The only thing I excelled at was track and field, and that was probably because I had learned to run away from students trying to beat me up or steal my shoes. I was the butt of every joke and couldn't understand why. Sadly, it was not so much about me being an immigrant, because my school had many other Iranian students, but primarily because I wasn't as masculine as the other boys. Sexuality was not talked about in Iran, so I had no clue what the school bullies were talking about when they called me a faggot or spewed any other slurs. Besides, I didn't speak English (or Spanish), so I just assumed they were calling me stupid or something of that nature. All I knew was that I was always the last person picked to be on every team, and my only friends were other outcasts who felt sorry for me. I hated my first years of school, but what I didn't know was that the abuse was about to escalate.

As the next few school years passed, I began to experience physical harassment and abuse by other male students. I wish it was just verbal harassment or at least the usual snatching of my backpack while forcing me to chase it only to have it thrown to someone farther away. Sometimes I gave up and later found it by my locker at the end of the day. By the end of seventh grade, the pushing, kicking, and ganging up became a regular hobby for even more kids. Word got out that this little boy did not know how to defend himself, so I became the school punching bag. It didn't matter how many times I complained to the school faculty, they always turned a blind eye. That left me no choice but to do the only thing I could come up with—flee!

On school days, I began to hide under my bed until my mom checked my room to make sure I left for

THE BEGINNING

school and then spent the rest of the day watching daytime television. I remember my mom being summoned to the office regarding my frequent absences and watching her shocked expression as she looked through the countless absent notes with her forged signature. In her broken English, she asked why I was skipping school, and when I told her and the Dean about the constant harassment, the Dean simply asked me to walk from one side of the office to the other and pointed out the way that I walked. He told my mother that my walk was too feminine, and it was expected for someone like me to be harassed. He also let us know that there was nothing he could do to prevent further harassment. My mother and I were speechless and, quite frankly, extremely helpless. The harassment continued to the point that the school year ended with me in the hospital due to an after-school altercation. I was kneed in the groin so hard that within a few days, one of my testicles had blown up to the size of a baseball and was eventually replaced by a saline implant. This is a scar I carry to this day.

THE CHARISMA WITHIN

The next year, I was lucky because my parents decided to move to a new area, giving me a chance to start all over again. I knew I had to try something new, or the previous year was going to be repeated all over again. I am certain that you can imagine how bad I wanted to be accepted by everyone around me, anyone for that matter, and in that attempt, I dimmed my light as a person and began to create alternate personas that I felt were more appealing to my peers. I began to lie about every aspect of my life. I lied so much that even my own private journal entries were nothing more than fiction. They were carefully crafted stories using bits and pieces of fictitious characters from all my favorite TV shows. I'm guessing everyone at school was very aware that I lived in a world of make belief but to me it felt safe. The beatings had stopped, but the harassment was still very much present. I could tolerate that type of harassment because I had begun to make some "friends" and no longer felt as alone. I would not call them friends now because I know they were just very shallow friendships, but it was better than

THE BEGINNING

nothing. I just remember hating my face, my body, and even worse, the person I was on the inside.

Later in this book, I will share the concepts I adopted to shift my entire way of thinking and become the person I am today. I look back at those dark times and do not recognize that eighth-grade teen who was envious of everyone he met, but I know now that without that period, I would not discover the formula that I will be sharing in this book. I later found the secret to becoming confident and charismatic. In a way, I am grateful for everything that I went through to gain the insight that I hope will help many to come.

There was a time when I would see charismatic people around me and envy them, but now I see them and feel closer to them than I ever have. I earned my true confidence from a place of having no confidence at all. I learned how to release doubt and pain and replace them with love and certainty. I changed very much in a short period of time, and though someone born with confidence and charisma could not explain to you how those things can be acquired, I can, and I will, because I learned to grow into it and later embody it with every fiber of my being. I know that my upbringing and challenged adolescence contributed greatly to my desire to learn the ability to enhance my confidence, but once I learned what I learned, nothing has given me more pleasure than to share what I have come to know. I know now that charisma can be learned and is not reserved for a select few. In my heart, I know that charisma can be taught, and I think I can teach it to anyone willing to listen and apply the things I have come to know.

It is time for us to become more of who we are and stop living in the shadows of false self-imagery. We are all special and unique, and it just takes a few shifts in the way that we think to tap into our true selves. I hope you will enjoy this journey with me. I wrote this book with the intention to make it as short and simple as possible because I wanted anyone to be able to read, comprehend, and apply these steps while seeing great results. Every single one of us deserves to be happy and surrounded by those who love us just the way we are, without falsehoods or fear of being rejected. So without further ado, I present my steps in enhancing your inner magnet.

"Your time is limited, so don't waste it living someone else's life. Don't be trapped by dogma — which is living with the results of other people's thinking."

STEVE JOBS

Step One:

MAKE PEACE WITH WHERE YOU ARE IN YOUR LIFE

Do not compare yourself with another, for there are no two people who are on an identical path.

I placed this step as the first step because I felt it to be the most important step of all. In our constant attempt to compare and judge our success with others, we tend to lose sight of our accomplishments and our victories. Generally, we do not give ourselves the credit that we deserve, especially for the many things we have successfully accomplished. We go about our lives only noticing our self-assessed and often miscalculated shortcomings only to devalue our inherent self-worth. The percentage of us guilty of miscalculating our self-worth is so high that I can basically say that, to some extent, it is pretty much everybody.

Most people tend to compare their success to those around them, trying to determine their self-worth solely through comparison. Though for some, that may be a way to feel better about themselves, for most, the comparisons cause us to feel inadequate and unworthy. I would not be so opposed to comparisons if there were solid and accurate ways to compare our success, but that is not, nor has ever been the case. If we had true and accurate measures, other than those imposed on us by our society, maybe to compare would have its benefits, but in the world that we live in, consistent measurements and standards do not exist. They are only what we have created for ourselves within every single society, and in each society, those standards vary. There are many false measurements, but at the top of the list is one misconception that deceives us the most, and that is financial success.

The worst misconception of them all is that our success is determined by our financial worth, and though it is great to be financially abundant, to determine our personal value based on the size of our bank account is undermining other very important aspects of our personality; aspects that play a much larger role in who we are as people. There are countless aspects of you that are evolving simultaneously at every moment, so to measure your value based on one aspect of your life can cloud the importance of the rest. Most of your successes are in fact mentally oriented and achieved within your mind as each day passes. You can compare yourself to the version of yourself that existed five years ago and notice how much your mind has developed in that period. Are you the same person you were five years ago? Can you honestly say yes? You can even look back a single year and see how much you have changed and learned in that small period. Are you the same person you were a year ago? I know I am not, and I don't think there is a single person in the world who ceases to grow each day with every waking moment of their life.

Every time you come to a new realization in life, or have an epiphany, you achieve a significant victory. A victory that is impossible to measure by standards given to us by any person or society. If you were to accurately measure your value, you must account for every one of those victories, as well as all the other things you typically deem important. As you already know, it is impossible to do that, so the mere attempt to determine self-worth based on material success is futile. It is my suggestion to accept that you are where you are and to accept that wherever that is, it is closer to your desired destination than ever before. Whether you feel that in the past you have been closer to any particular goal or not, understand that all that you have lived so far has caused you to become who you are at this moment, and you have never been better equipped than you are today to be able to sustain any success that you wish to acquire.

Past failures teach us lessons and cause us to grow. Past successes teach us lessons and cause us to grow as well. Unless you have been in a coma since the day of your birth, you have been growing each day and getting closer to everything you have ever wanted to be. That is why it is important to accept the value of the current position in your personal path to self-realization. Love where you are today because without today, tomorrow is not possible. But the one thing that this step helps you with the most is to point you in the direction of your success. Because it is only through your acceptance and appreciation of where you are at this moment that it is possible to become aware of the pathways that lead to your ultimate journey and ensure that you are pointed in the right direction.

It is the judgment and condemnation of where you are and how you ended up here that keeps you from reaching your full potential. You are more now than you have ever been before, and everything that you have lived has contributed to the person you are today. See your life and your past as a priceless path that has led you here, to a place that is new and full of potential. Take the good that you have lived and be thankful for it. Now take the bad that you have lived and be thankful for that too. The good might have felt better, but the bad and difficult times have more power to shape your character than any good or easy time of your life. Mistakes cannot be avoided, and don't worry, you will make many more mistakes by the time you end your journey in this life, so don't punish yourself for it. Don't punish another for it.

We are experts at making mistakes and enhancing our growth because of the lessons we learn in the process. Mistakes help us grow, but most importantly, they also enhance our ability to appreciate all that we have. It is only when we look at ourselves as a whole and not judge our past, or be victimized by it, that we can truly accept and appreciate where we are now. And in order to do that, you need to make peace with where you are in your life at this moment.

Never judge yourself or your place in life because you DO NOT have the ability to judge accurately. Nobody does! And remember to never compare yourself with another, for there are no two people who are on an identical path. Every person begins life with different circumstances; some have seemingly huge advantages, some have huge disadvantages, and others are somewhere in between. What you must do now is to accept that you are on your path and decide to not judge your place on the path. For in the mere acceptance of your place on the path that is your life, you have now advanced your position and enhanced your inner magnetism.

"Success is not final; failure is not fatal: It is the courage to continue that counts."

WINSTON S. CHURCHILL

"You have been criticizing yourself for years and it hasn't worked. Try approving of yourself and see what happens."

LOUISE HAY

Step Two:

MAKE PEACE WITH YOUR BODY

Focus on parts you love and give no attention to parts you do not.

In the beginning, for most people, this next step is not an easy one. I have had (and still have) lots of issues with this topic. The way we view our bodies is an extremely important part of who we are as a person. Feeling uneasy about one's physical appearance can be extremely taunting and damaging to our state of mind. As a result, any habitual negative views of our body could potentially harm endless aspects of our lives. The way we view ourselves is so important that I had to make sure this step came second. Ironically, this is one area that even the most beautiful people in the world seem to have issues with.

Due to my years of experience in the first chapter of my life as a makeup artist, I have acquired a lot of insight on this topic. Whether at a makeup event at a department store or backstage at a fashion show, I have found that most people seem to be extremely critical of their outward appearance. I don't think I have ever come across anyone, even supermodels, who have been able to look at themselves in the mirror and not pick out a flaw. It took me a long time to realize that it was not just me asking myself the question, "Am I attractive?" It was just about anyone I ever met. There are those who are, by current media standards, commonly accepted as beautiful and those people are more often reassured by their beauty than the rest. Yet even those traditional beauties have an expiration date.

STEP TWO

In comparison to an average life span, conventional beauty is extremely short lived. Once the awkward teenage years come to pass, most people peak for approximately ten to twenty years before time and gravity begin to take their toll. A few are fortunate enough to ride out their beauty for many decades, but they are a small minority. Fortunately, beauty is truly in the eyes of the beholder, and as cliché as that may sound, each person recognizes beauty in their own personal and unique way. Chances are, we won't look at ourselves and see the all-around beauty that someone else might see. But in my experience, there is always someone who will see the beauty in you, even if you don't see it yourself. Just think of the last time you saw a beautiful, wrinkled, gray-haired person and were impressed with the radiant glow of their personality. Authentic beauty is everywhere, but it takes the right person to be able to see it. This is also true in terms of relationships, there is always someone for everyone, and there is always somebody who has been spending their entire life looking just for you.

THE CHARISMA WITHIN

It is not possible to be beautiful in everyone's eyes, and even those media-celebrated beauties are not considered beautiful by everyone. I remember when I was growing up, darker skin and larger lips were not considered beautiful. My sister was teased about her darker skin tone and her larger lips, but now it seems that everyone wants to spend all their time tanning their skin and getting injected with some chemical to make their lips look larger. The things that she was teased about are now admired attributes. But unfortunately, someone who has been teased their entire life might still consider their larger lips a flaw and their tanned skin unwanted. I could not tell you how many people I have met who tried to make their beautiful large lips look smaller through a particular style of lining the lips or the color of a lipstick. There are many cultures that consider a full figure more beautiful than a thin build and vice versa.

I know when I gain more weight, my family starts to tell me that I look great, while my peers start to drop hints implying that it is time to go back on a better exercise regimen. It is always the same story; once I lose some weight, my mother starts asking me to start eating because I am beginning to look like I have been starving for weeks, and my friends start telling me that I look great. At times, it can be confusing whose opinion to follow, but most importantly, it is important to realize that they are just opinions and nothing more. During our lifetime, it is in our minds that we record those standards imposed upon us by the people in our environment. Once we are programmed, it takes a tremendous amount of effort to erase the false programming that has not been serving us. It becomes very difficult to change our standards on our own.

Every decade, the masses decide on a new set of standards, and the new standards become somewhat contagious. What most people think is beautiful is in a constant state of flux, and you can see the evidence of that when you look at fashion or makeup trends. For example, in my lifetime, I have witnessed the female eyebrows being admired for their un-groomed and large nature to being pencil thin and plucked to high heaven. Then the eyebrows grew back again a bit larger and shapely, and now once again, the recent trend is huge eyebrows that are overfilled, long, and feathered. And that was just the eyebrows. There have not been two decades that held the same standards for beauty. In order to please everyone, you must have a complete body replacement surgery about every ten years. The only escape from the endless cycle is to take a moment, step back from your current perspective, and accept that the concept of beauty is constantly changing, and there is no catching up with it. Once you adopt the new trends, the standards change, and that leaves you with two choices; to jump through the new hoops or make peace with where you are.

Making peace with your body does not mean letting go of the desire for improvement. I am not saying that we should not try to improve and maintain our physical body, instead I am suggesting making every

STEP TWO

improvement with a positive attitude. Many people are driven to self-improvement (i.e., exercise or diet) from a place of self-loathing and hatred with no regard for its health benefits. I do not see that as a healthy state of being in any possible way, and it is not a great starting point by any means. It is definitely a motivating factor but not a healthy or a sustainable one. I know that at times, I have decided to go to the gym after a look in the mirror that caused much self-hatred, but the process was always an awkward and unfulfilling experience. Going to the gym mad or upset does not reap you the best results. Oftentimes, you lose some weight and then start to eat again and end up right where you started, but this time maybe at a worse place than the one you started from.

Starting any project from a negative standpoint seldom leads to great results. Our attitude prior to any self-improvement is extremely important. We can see the evidence of that with many people in our society. Think of people who have plastic surgery. If the surgery is done from a place of low self-confidence and extreme insecurity, the addiction for the surgery begins, and I am certain that you have seen many people end up looking cartoonish and artificial! Now, there are many confident people that use plastic surgery as a form of an upgrade, or maintenance, and end up with great results. It is the same with diet and exercise. Actions taken with a positive attitude rooted in confidence, and self-love always reap the best rewards.

There is also another way to look at yourself when you feel that there is something physical that needs improvement. Instead of looking at yourself in the mirror and triggering self-loathing, see your body in its improved state, and you'd be surprised by the success you can have in achieving it. Look at the part bothering you, and with your mind's eye, see how you would prefer it to be. Because only when you stop the self-loathing process, the true improvement begins. This can be a very effective exercise. Seeing yourself as you wish to be also triggers excitement and hope, and that

STEP TWO

is the best possible attitude to have prior to attempting any action toward self-improvement.

The worst thing to ever do is to find one thing about your body (your appearance) that you do not like and fixate on it. Once again, I am the poster child for this type of behavior. The repercussions can be very damaging. When you fixate on one spot, you lose perspective and your ability to be objective. Many people who are anorexic can tell you that they only see a tiny pocket of fat on one spot of their body, and in their attempt to get rid of that single spot, they begin to look extremely thin and unhealthy in other parts of their body. But once you lose perspective, you cannot see distortions of the other parts of the body, yet you still see the tiny pocket of fat that due to your attention never tends to go away. When someone thin says, "I'm fat," they are often referring to the one spot that they obsess over. For some, this is hard to understand but I am sure many can relate. The same concepts also apply to the obsessions of the "junk in the trunk" or oversized breasts. People have surgeries and injections to achieve huge "assets," but often disproportionate to the rest of their body. When fixated on one spot, people lose objectivity and stop seeing their image as a whole but instead a singular part. The moment most people glance into the mirror, their attention goes to one certain spot and that spot is seldom their best feature. I am sure if those people saw a black silhouette of their bodies from multiple angles, they might have a different perspective but that is never the case because most people see their self-assessed flaws using tunnel vision.

With the understanding of this step, hopefully that can change because awareness is essential for improvement. This step is not much different than the previous because it is about acceptance and our ability to let go of the harsh critic that lives inside us all. Though it is impossible to stop evaluating our current state of being, for it is through that process that the desire for growth is even possible, it is very important to make peace with where we are at this moment and be easy on yourself.

When it comes to our physical bodies, it seems a bit more challenging, but the advice that I must give is one that I was given by a great teacher and that was to find a body part that you love about yourself and put your primary focus on that part and that part alone. As for the other parts that you are not so crazy about, first understand that it could be worse, regardless of your situation!!! Then once you feel a little better about those areas, put your focus back on the areas that you do like about yourself. This is a bit difficult at first, but with little practice, it can become second nature. The other incentive is that when you start to appreciate any part of yourself, other people begin to take notice as well. You will hear comments made on those areas that you feel good about. Luckily, the way that this world works is that once you start getting accustomed to appreciating any part of who you are, the things to appreciate seem to multiply, and those who appreciate you seem to multiply as well.

If at this moment, you feel that there is nothing you can appreciate about your body, take your focus off the appearance of your body and put your attention on the inner workings of the fully functional genius system that is your body. There are so many aspects of your body you can appreciate that you would need an entire lifetime to go through every part of your body that is functioning properly, even if you are very sick. The cells of our bodies are continuously at work, doing their best in any given situation, and that is basically the same process that we need to adopt. We need to take our situation and make the best of it until the situation improves, and if you maintain that type of attitude, improvement is not that far away. Once again, if what you do not like about yourself is not something that could be improved upon, take your focus off it completely because there is nothing you can do at this moment but find other areas that you can appreciate. Focusing on the unchangeable brings nothing but

STEP TWO

stress, sadness, and anxiety. But it is not until you take the step to find something about yourself to appreciate that any improvement is remotely possible.

Make the effort and find something that you love about yourself. Find it, obsess on it, and love it. Once you begin doing that, you will see that self-appreciation can open doors that you never imagined possible.

"Take criticism seriously, not personally. If there is truth or merit in the criticism, try to learn from it. Otherwise, let it roll right off of you."

HILLARY CLINTON

Step Three:

DETACH FROM CRITICISM AND PRAISE

Understand that no one's opinion has any bearing on your self-worth.

Although there may be great benefit to positive or negative feedback, I recommend not getting too attached to compliments or criticism for they are nothing but opinions filtered through each individual's standards and beliefs. There are no two people that hold the exact same standards or beliefs. Obviously, my intention by writing this book is self-improvement and with that mindset, constructive criticism can have great benefits, but even in those cases, it is very important for you to understand that another's opinion of you has very little to do with you. I know that sounds far-fetched, but it is a fact. This is extremely important for you to understand.

Each of us sees life through our own eyes and can only perceive as much as we are able based on our unique personal programming. Our ability to perceive is mostly based upon our own life experience, adopted personal standards, and shared values. Each person has a different set of previous, and extremely individual, life experiences, so how each person perceives another (person or situation) is solely dependent on the perceiver and the perceiver alone. Even the standards that we feel we have in common are not identically interpreted. We tend to see the world through our own eyes and are only sensitive to things that have personal meaning to us. This statement is a very important statement that needs extra attention to assure its comprehension. I think the best way I can explain it is

STEP THREE

through the simplest examples. I will start with our appearance, because it is the first thing people notice when they see us.

Let's say that you have had an acne problem your entire life, and I have had issues with dark circles around my eyes, and we walk into a room filled with a handful of people. Your eyes will automatically scan the faces of everyone to analyze their skin texture, and my attention will be drawn to the area surrounding each person's eyes. You could find someone who has dark circles under their eyes but no blemishes and consider their face beautiful and I would do the opposite. Chances are, if you do not have issues or a history with a particular topic, you are not going to notice it as much; therefore, you will be less likely to make a comment (internal or external). Now if we notice something and feel obliged to comment, it is usually because of our own previous history with the topic at hand. Another example is if you had a spouse with a tendency to procrastinate, you might become more sensitive to mismanaged time and notice anyone who in your opinion is a procrastinator. And someone else will not notice or be bothered by the same issue. These are just a few tiny examples, but the list is endless.

You rarely notice things that do not have specific meaning to you. Instead, what you notice when you look around has more to do with your personal interpretation than the thing you are observing. In the same regards, when someone else looks at you and makes a comment, that comment is being made based upon that person's unique history. It has nothing to do with you, even though the comment is aimed directly at you. You just happen to be the catalyst for the train of thoughts triggered in that person's mind. This concept is particularly difficult for some people to understand, because a lot of people take comments extremely personally, even when they are not directly aimed at them. But it is wise to understand that another person's view of you has very little to do with you, whether it is negative or positive.

Imagine wearing a red sweater and meeting two unrelated people whose parents wore red sweaters all the time. But one of those people had abusive parents and the other had very loving parents. Do you think that both people will react the same way to your sweater or the person wearing that sweater? Do you think their opinion of your sweater makes your sweater better or worse in any way? Or makes you better or worse? Of course not! I think this is a great general example to explain what I mean when I say that you should not make anyone's comments personal.

In all honesty, I have to say that this step is a little tricky because it needs constant reminding. I believe not being attached to compliments is a much easier task than letting go of criticism. Although I might be wrong because every person's thought process and priority is different. I couldn't tell you which takes longer because each case is completely different.

Though I can tell you about the stage that I am in at this moment, and it is a much more advanced place than when I started. I love the fact that in life, regardless of what it is you are learning, there is always room to advance. If I were to tell you that I have completely mastered it, I would be lying. So here I am being as honest as I can be to help you understand the step better. I have become very good at detaching myself from other people's opinions, but sometimes, it just takes a little extra effort.

When it comes to positive feedback, I appreciate it very much, and then I find that the appreciation moves towards the kindness of the person delivering it. I don't let it get me so excited that it begins to define me. Though I must admit that I am so wired into feeling good most of the time that I will use anything as an excuse to feel better. I try to milk every positive moment, because if I don't, I will lose an opportunity to experience more momentary joy. But the key word is momentary, and being aware of that, I don't think of it as something extremely important. I do think that riding the high of a momentary joy is extremely valuable for the sake of living life to the fullest, but the attachment to it is what has the potential to create a problem. Usually, if I receive a compliment, I say "thank you," smile, and a few moments later, I will forget all about it, because I understand that if ten people were to make comments on this same subject, it would be impossible for all feedback to come back positive. So you can say that I appreciate having encountered a person who has something positive to say about me, and in that moment, I draw a level of joy. But the feeling of detachment is still there.

It is important to let your own feelings and opinions be your main guide. If I were to start a project that I loved and believed in strongly, I would not back down and reevaluate the project because of a few naysayers. It is one thing to be uncertain of something and put it out for feedback, but this example is of something that I strongly believe in and feel good about. In most cases,

THE CHARISMA WITHIN

I will have to let my feelings be my guide, not another's opinions. Now let's go a little deeper in the negative arena, because that is where most people have trouble being detached. Here are a few examples of how I deal with negative feedback. I will give actual examples instead of making them generic in order to be more specific.

About fifteen years ago, I worked at a department store, and I eagerly stepped into my manager's office wanting to show her photos of the Christmas party we had all attended the night before. When I walked in, I saw her on the phone checking her messages and patiently sat in a chair opposite her bursting with excitement and energy. As I started to scan through the photos in my camera, I realized that checking her message was taking longer than I thought. As I was trying to decide whether I should stay or leave, she turned to me using a very stern and irritated tone and said, "Go outside! This is not the time or the place for that!" You should have seen me, I felt like a child

STEP THREE

whose bad behavior had just caused him to be severely reprimanded. I know that looking back now I can see that it wasn't that big of a deal, but at that moment, I felt like a nuisance and that hurt every fiber of my being. You wouldn't think that one small (and not so negative) comment could hurt so much, but I know it was mostly because of how high I was feeling and how fast I came crashing down.

As I began walking toward my workstation, I realized that something outside of me had caused my mood to descend and that made me feel very uncomfortable. I immediately decided that I wanted the uncomfortable moment to stay just that, a moment and nothing more. So I began the now-familiar process of talking myself out of a negative feeling. I told myself that had I walked into that same office with the same attitude and found her in a different mood, the outcome would be different. Just the mere acknowledgment of that fact made me feel better, so I decided to take it to the next level and find someone who shared my excitement for these photos, and I did. It wasn't long before my employer had found me and not only apologized for her stern tone but also was enthusiastic about seeing the photos. That was when I realized that when she said, "This is not the time or the place for that!" that she really meant to say, "This is not a good time." There was no reason for me to be so hurt by that comment. There was no way I could've known that it was bad timing unless she told me so. Her stern voice had made me feel like I had done something wrong, when in fact, it was just not the time for that, and had I not talked myself out of that negative feeling, I could have still felt bad about myself. I guess the key was to recognize that I didn't like the feeling I was experiencing and made a conscious effort to change it.

Now I am going to show you my progress regarding positive feedback. Here is how I have changed over time regarding compliments. At first, a compliment made me feel very good, and it gave me a high; then I went out of my way to outdo whatever it was I did and

STEP THREE

seek more compliments. Then I concluded that I needed to detach myself from the compliment, and it didn't matter whether people said something nice to (or about) me or not. I would still appreciate the words of kindness, but no longer rushed to outdo myself to fish for more compliments. Later, the feeling became slightly less amazing, but my appreciation for the person's kindness started to deepen and that was amazing in its own way.

Once upon a time, this step would be most important regarding opinions of those close to us, but the age of social media makes this step also relevant to feedback from total strangers. The number of followers, "likes," and comments are becoming more valuable than they should ever be. People read comments by many strangers and let it affect their entire day, or worse, their opinion of self. They even make drastic changes to themselves or opinions to receive more positive feedback. That is why this step is more important now than ever. We must, as a collective, begin to detach ourselves from other people's opinions and approval. Our value must come from within and not the other way around.

"You are free. You are powerful. You are good. You are love. You have value. You have purpose. All is well."

ESTHER HICKS

Step Four:

KNOW YOUR INHERENT VALUE

You are contributing greatly to this world through your individuality, and you are connected to the same intelligence that runs the entire universe.

It's very easy to forget that we are born with an immense amount of value. It doesn't matter if we accomplish a single thing in our lives, just the fact that we are souls in a living body makes us special and extremely valuable. We are born at an exceptional time in the bodies of an incredibly unique species on this very lucky planet. Whether we feel it or not, we are extremely special and live in an extraordinary moment in human history. Humanity has never experienced more freedom and access to realize its potential. Regardless of the countless injustices in the world, our ancestors had much more difficult lives than we do. We have more opportunities as individuals to thrive than ever before. But the key is to believe in ourselves and constantly remind ourselves that we are, in fact, worthy. It sounds simple but sometimes it is easier said than done. The following are two major concepts that help me every single day in remembering my self-worth.

First Concept:

It is not hard to understand that the thing that makes this world so wonderful is its diversity. It is through the blend of each individual's unique self-expression that this world is formed. Think of the

STEP FOUR

magnificence of the evening sky. It is the intense glow of each individual star that contributes mightily to the beauty of all that is visible. Each star plays an equal and significant role in the creation of that breathtaking view. In our world, we are not that different from those stars, but what makes us shine is our uniqueness. We, as individuals, will only be able to maximize our contribution to the world if we shine as brightly as we are able. It is important to know that each star is extremely significant, and what you can offer this world (regardless of how big or small) can only be contributed by you and you alone.

You are one of a kind, and there is no one else in this world who is exactly like you. The more of you that you allow to surface, the more this world benefits. I believe these steps are great ways to allow the real you to surface. Understanding the importance of that is extremely crucial because it is not only you who will reap the benefit of your efforts, but also the entire planet. You might not be someone in a position to influence on a global scale, but you are very capable of adding to the sweetness of diversity. The more of you that you allow to shine, the richer we become as a society. I feel that it is very important to understand that we do influence this world, even if we only live simple lives. I do believe that if we do not let our true selves shine, the world will be a lesser place. The more you shine, the more magnificent the world becomes, and more people around you will be able to benefit from your existence. I believe that through the understanding of this step, you can regain a lot of your unrealized self-worth and begin to understand your true value, a value that is yours alone. A value that no one can ever take from you. You are of great value, and you contribute greatly to this universe.

The world was not the same before your arrival, and it is very important for you to know that it will never be the same after your departure. You are making this world more than it has ever been, and you should feel special about that. You are important and so is

STEP FOUR

everyone else. Just remember that you, me, and every other person in this world is adding greatly to the whole picture through our individuality, but how brightly we shine is completely up to each and every one of us.

It feels as if we should all already know this. That we should all know our value in this world, but unfortunately, that is not the case. We are taught that we must mature and achieve huge accomplishments to make the slightest difference, and that we have nothing to offer unless we are successful in our professions influencing the world on a huge scale. Those who are highly accomplished are of great value to this world, but even those who are not as "accomplished" are contributing as well. There is no way to compare someone who lives a public and influential life with someone who leads a simple life. Both are contributing differently, and both elements are required to make this world what it is. No one can ever say that one is more important than the other, but you should definitely know that both are just as important.

Second Concept:

I remember being a teenager and feeling small and inferior. My inferiority was not in comparison to others but in contrast to nature. I would look at animals and see how perfectly they migrate and how intelligent they are. I would see our solar system and be in awe of how perfectly the planets orbit the sun. I would stare at the flowers and wonder how they knew when to bloom and then find myself going through the same process with the trees. . . I could go on forever. All of them knew their role in this world and knew what to do and when to do it. But I didn't!!!

I didn't understand how my little brain was supposed to compete with such divine intelligence. At that time, I felt very small and unworthy, but with time, I realized how wrong I had been. As years passed, I found myself in many different situations and

STEP FOUR

dilemmas, where my conscious thinking mind could not comprehend and/or fathom a solution. But somehow, my instincts would kick in and get me out of what seemed like a conundrum. There are many times I had the impulse to get up and go somewhere only to find myself at the perfect place at the perfect time, or many almost fatal accidents that would freak my mother out, where she would say, "If we had crossed this intersection one second earlier, we would all be dead!!!"

I have had countless perfect impulses to be late or early, or to keep my mouth shut, or to speak up, that I know there is an inner voice that is always speaking to each of us. Regardless of the situation, there is always the impulse to do the perfect thing but only when we are tuned into it. When it came to the nearly fatal accidents, my mother always freaked out for days thinking how lucky we were and how something outside of us must have saved us. But as I became more aware, I realized that our savior was our connection to the same intelligence that I had been envious of my entire life. The same intelligence that governs the universe and keeps it running so perfectly was also a part of me, or I, a part of it. I realized that I was not alone and not insignificant in the least bit but a part of something huge. You can only imagine how much my self-worth increased after that realization. When necessary, my instincts would kick in and take care of everything. I realized how much I must be relying on my instincts without ever realizing it. It is impossible to determine how many accidents I didn't get into or how many bad things I have unknowingly avoided. I do know that we are all linked to each other, to the outside world, and to the universe. With us being a part of something so huge, I realized that we must be significant as well. How significant? I do not know. But one thing I do know is that we are not insignificant, because we are part of this entire magical universe.

We are all important. We all add to the diversity and perfection of this universe. And we are very much

STEP FOUR

tapped into the indefinable and infinite intelligence that governs this world.

Every time I feel small or forget my value, I repeat those statements over and over until I have been fully reminded of them. It is important to not just believe those statements but also to know when to remind yourself of them. As much as you might come to believe in any of these steps, you must know that you will not always remember them, and there will be many occasions where you will need to remind yourself. All of us tend to get caught up in the moment forgetting important ideas that are of great benefit. That is why a book like this can come in handy and is important to remind us of the things we might forget. Just reading a book like this one time isn't as valuable as if you keep it near and reread the parts that you are drawn to, or need reminding of.

"Never live to impress anyone...You will only get their attention...Live to express yourself...Trust me...People will respect you..."

TEJAS PATIL

Step Five:

NEVER TRY TO IMPRESS ANYONE WITH MORE THAN YOU ARE

Decide that you'd rather be surrounded by a few people who know and love the real you than surrounded by many people who love you for a false idealistic image that you portray.

This step is probably more relevant now than when I originally wrote it fifteen years ago. It is a concept that changed my life forever, and now to my surprise, I am

THE CHARISMA WITHIN

surrounded by quite a large group of friends and acquaintances, but all of whom know, love, and respect the real me. Now let's go back to my past and revisit the insecure unhappy eighth-grade version of me that I mentioned in the beginning of this book. I know that my story of trying to fit in by spewing constant lies is a much more exaggerated version of most other stories I hear, but I feel that it explains how I came to believe in the power of this step. So here is a brief refresher of the time I mentioned earlier when I was not comfortable with who I was and the things that were brewing inside of me. In fact, I was so uncomfortable that I was not even aware of the person I was on the inside. I had grown so accustomed to expressing myself only in the ways that I wished to be viewed, that I would seldom attempt to look inside.

At the time, I was an immigrant teenager trying to master the English language and a queer boy who had no idea what the word queer meant (this was 1992). I was different in every possible way. I was not rich,

STEP FIVE

didn't feel attractive, didn't fit in, didn't fully comprehend the culture or the world that I had been thrown into, but I needed to find a way to make people like me. I would lie and pretend to be anyone other than the person I was on the inside. The surface layers of me were being designed by my own ego for the sole purpose of impressing others. I wanted to look good, I wanted to be loved, and in that attempt, I had made a lot of acquaintances who liked the version of me that they were presented with. I made up stories that would make me look cool and better than I felt I was. But deep inside, I always felt a lack, and to fill it, I would try to further impress and make more "friends."

It was my last year in that specific middle school because we were once again moving to a new part of town. And as people were signing my yearbook, I had no idea what a profound lesson I was about to learn from their meaningless words. When I looked at the many signatures I had received that year and read what my friends had written, as sweet as they attempted to be, their words were empty. I must admit that in the attempt to keep, make, and maintain those friends, I had grown hollow and exhausted. So exhausted, that I decided that the following year was going to be different. I was not going to try and impress anybody. I told myself that when the time came and I was about to make my next friend, I was going to be completely honest with my new possible friends and show my imperfections.

You can imagine what a scary attempt that was because the prior year, I had been severely hurt by not standing up for myself. A lot had changed in that year, and eighth grade was not as brutal but still empty. I told myself that once again, I was given a do-over. So sick of pretending to be someone I was not, I decided to simply not care how I came across. I wanted to see if there was a chance to make some real friends. To my surprise, I found the courage, stuck to my guns, and followed through with my decision. At first, it was very difficult to catch myself and I would constantly fall

STEP FIVE

back into my old habits of misrepresenting the truth, but I did not give up. I decided that I was no longer going to try and impress the people around me. I even came out as "bisexual" even though there were no other out students in the entire school. I was the very first! In the previous years, I didn't know what I was, but that year, someone explained to me that some people are attracted to their own sex. The LGBTQ community had very little representation in the nineties, and the small amounts of information that we knew of "those" people were always negative, related to mental corruption, and AIDS. Yet, the moment I heard about the concept of being queer, I immediately resonated with it, and with my new pact of telling the truth decided to not deny any part of myself regardless of how scary as it may seem.

I will never forget the moment when word got around my new school that I was not straight. I distinctly remember mobs of people asking me questions as I tried to answer them as honestly as possible. I stood my ground, stayed true to the person I was on the inside, and answered every possible question. Eventually, the excitement faded and changed my life forever.

That was a humongous departure from my old self, and at the end of that year, I had made some amazing friends, a few of which I am still very close to. I remember wiping my joyous tears as I was reading what everyone had written at the end of that year in my yearbook. I was so touched by everyone's kind and sincere words that I burst into tears. I don't think I had ever felt as loved by my friends as I did at that moment. I remember how many people expressed their admiration of my courage to be myself. That year felt as if people were drawn to me for the real me, and I always wondered what they would think of me if they knew me the year before. I felt wonderful, and as great as that felt, I realized that through expressing myself without restriction, I learned more about myself than I ever knew possible. I was more in touch with myself

STEP FIVE

and that felt even better than making all those wonderful friends. That was when I promised myself that I would always be open and honest about every aspect of my personality whether it made me proud or embarrassed. I would never try to impress anyone ever again by pretending to be someone I was not. I would just be myself, and if people found what I had to offer impressive, it was because they genuinely were impressed. I appreciated the value of true friendship more than ever and I wanted nothing less. Though I must say that because of the success I experienced, I found it extremely easy to keep my promise. That was the year that I realized that I would rather be surrounded by just a few people who loved me, for the real me, than a lot of people who didn't know me at all. That was the year I broke generations of tradition and started my own.

I believe that the most reward in any friendship comes when the connection is on a deeper level. Those are the friendships that make our lives richer and allow us to experience love like never before. I understood that the deeper connections are not possible if there are guards up in the friendship. Unless you are both comfortable being yourself in front of the other, the connection stays superficial. The deeper the connection, the more gratifying it feels and the less you feel alone in this world. There is nothing like knowing that you are not alone, and that there are people out there who care about you, just the way you are. Not having to impress anyone feels good, and ironically, in being true to who you are, you end up impressing everyone without trying.

I do have to admit that it is a lot easier for a teenager switching schools to try to reinvent themselves and not quite as easy for an adult who has years of practice concealing and protecting their inner flaws, but the journey is still the same. As an adult, it requires a lot of courage to chip away at the small aspects of yourself that you have created to fit in or feel accepted. It's nearly impossible to just wake up and be your most authentic self, but for now, you can start becoming aware of the parts of you that are not as authentic.

Decide that you will slowly and comfortably start to reveal your true self to everyone around you. Tell yourself that even one true friend is better than ten acquaintances. Be honest with yourself and honest with everyone you encounter, and do not fear any negative consequence. There is no real negative consequence to being your most authentic self. At first, you might feel as if you are alienating certain people, but trust me, you could never alienate a true friend by being yourself. Only those who are no longer a match to the new you will leave your experience, and in their place, you will find new people who appreciate you to the fullest. When you begin to be as real as you can possibly be, you will notice that people will automatically be drawn to you. It is a great contributor to your inner magnet. This is one step that you cannot skip, because without it you will not see significant results.

"Associate yourself with people of good quality, for it is better to be alone than in bad company."

BOOKER T. WASHINGTON

Step Six:

BE PICKY CHOOSING YOUR FRIENDS

Decide that you would rather be surrounded by people who are true to themselves and flawed, than those who present themselves as flawless.

Though this step falls naturally into place when you begin to practice the last, it is still very important for you to make a deliberate shift in your own consciousness. Once you decide in a more deliberate manner, the results will come forth much faster. As you are becoming more of who you really are, you will automatically start to attract people of the same nature. That is great to know because it makes your work much easier. But there is still work for you to do. Your work is to decide that genuine and flawed is much more appealing than misrepresented perfection. If you can say that and mean it, you are far along your way.

It is also important for you to know that by making this decision, you are not lowering your standards in what you want in a friend or an acquaintance but instead raising them. I am not saying that you should seek people with flaws, I am just saying that you should seek people who are genuine and comfortable exposing their imperfections and insecurities. It just so happens that when your friends are more genuine, you are more likely to know about their flaws. People who are truly genuine are less likely to hold back and hide their shortcomings in order to impress you.

It is important to be picky about the kind of people

STEP SIX

you choose to spend your time with. I have witnessed many occasions when people are new to a location and in order to avoid loneliness, they befriend anyone who seems interested. That goes for romantic relationships as well. If someone is interested and somewhat attractive, they become a viable candidate. Well, that doesn't always work out for the best, but it is not a complete loss either, even those situations have something to offer. They can be a great way to get to know what characteristics you prefer (and not prefer) in the people you surround yourself with. Life is a growing experience, and I would be wrong to say that you should not follow through with a mutual attraction (whether a friendship or relationship). In those situations, the problems often arise when people hold on to people for the sole reason of having more friends or for the fear of being lonely. But if your intention is to find someone who is genuine and has many things in common with you, you will soon know whether you should continue with that connection or not.

THE CHARISMA WITHIN

We all have great instincts letting us know how appropriate any situation or person is for us at that moment. If your goal is to have as many friends as possible, your instincts will only guide you to having more friends, regardless of how good that friend is for you. But if you clarify what it is you want in a friend and start with trying to find quality not quantity, you will be amazed at how much your instincts will begin to guide you to exactly what it is you are seeking. But you must be clear about what you want.

The specifics are up to you, but the one thing that I urge you to put at the very top of your list is AUTHENTICITY. Don't worry about the rest! Your instincts will always guide you to the right people and you will come to realize how pleasant it is to be surrounded by those who have nothing to hide. It's like a breath of fresh air in a smoggy town. It also gives you a great sense of security. But I must express one important fact, you must also be in a place where you are trying to be true to yourself because you cannot

STEP SIX

attract and keep anyone who is genuine unless you are trying to be genuine yourself.

I know some would say, "well, isn't everyone trying to be genuine in one way or another?" There are many people in this world who try to be genuine with some but also have their not-so-genuine moments with others. For example, there are many that do not care about the quality of a person's character and only befriend them for what they can receive from that person. That happens quite a lot in this world, but hardly anyone is willing to admit it. It often happens with people with some sort of power, ranging from the bouncers at an event (helping them get into a prestigious party), producers in Hollywood, politicians, and so much more. Some people try too hard to form a bond (whether fake or real) without caring if there is common ground between them and the people they are befriending. They are only interested in what they can get out of the connection, not what they are able to offer. What those people don't understand is that usually the person they are trying to befriend will read them like a book. Their words might sound perfect and genuine, but their energy tells a different tale. People are not stupid. Some people might not be very quick witted or street smart, but everyone can read energy regardless of their IQ. On a deep yet subtle level, people always know what your intentions are before you even open your mouth. I am not saying that you should not try to meet people and make connections that will help you in a particular way, but it's important to remember that even in forming those advantageous relationships, you can still be genuine.

Personally, I know many people that I only contact for specific reasons. But I never feign a friendship where there is none. We talk about what we are there to talk about, have something to offer, and we get on with business. The point that I am making is to be genuine even in situations that sometimes are not that "genuine." Don't fake anything! Pretending to like someone, when you don't, for a desired outcome will

STEP SIX

only chip away at your own magnetic quality. Just be yourself and you will always get the things that you want but instead through someone who is a better match to you.

There are many different circumstances, and I can give enough examples to fill an entire book, but let's get down to the basics and do the work that needs to be done to attract the right kind of person. Your work is to decide what kind of people you prefer to be around. You can start by making the statement that you would prefer to be surrounded by more genuine people. Oftentimes, making statements such as that is all the work that needs to be done. It reminds you of what is important to you, and by doing that, who you attract changes. You can even take it one step further and make a list of the qualities you would like in your friends. If you have friends who have lied to you in the past, just write, "I would like to meet honest people." Don't focus so much on the negative because every time you focus on negative qualities, you decrease the power of your inner magnet and that becomes very counterproductive. Just make a list (short or long) of the qualities you'd like to see in your friends. Making that list has many benefits, but most importantly, it reminds you of what is important to you, and surprisingly, it will also remind you of the things you'd like to see in yourself as a friend. Start making the list now before you go to the next step, because you might forget if you don't. Come back and continue reading when you are done with your list.

Another great suggestion when you enter a friendship is having the mindset of what it is YOU have to offer and not what you can gain from the other. If your focus is on how you can contribute to your friendships, not what you can gain from them, the friendships naturally become more satisfying. I know some will assume that with that attitude, you put yourself at the risk of being used, but what often happens is that you meet other people with similar intentions and mindsets. They are there to be of service

STEP SIX

just as much as you are. If that premise is at your core, you give off the energy that allows you to find true friendships that last a lifetime. In this process, it will also become evident that many people who you meet are just temporary acquaintances and nothing more.

At the same time, be aware of the intentions of others and make friends with people who have the same core values. As I already mentioned, if both people are trying to make friendships so they can contribute in a mutual fashion, then your bond can grow and last. But if you enter a friendship with ulterior motives, your impure intentions begin to immediately taint the foundation of what could otherwise be a great partnership.

"I like flaws and feel more comfortable around people who have them. I myself am made entirely of flaws, stitched together with good intentions."

AUGUSTEN BURROUGHS

Step Seven:

MAKE A DECISION TO RELEASE THE GUARDS THAT HIDE YOUR FLAWS

Make it okay to be vulnerable.

There is not a single person that walks this earth who has not been plagued by insecurities at one time or another. Sometimes we feel that we are the only ones in the world that doubt countless aspects of ourselves, but the truth is that we are not alone. Humanity is more similar than different and the one thing you can count on is that we are all full of flaws, whether real or imagined. Oftentimes, those flaws are nothing more than made-up personal demons having a field day in our minds. They break us down and make us feel vulnerable. It is easy to fall into the trap of wondering how anyone can like, or even love, someone who has so many insecurities and flaws. It is very natural for us to want to appear strong. The built-in human survival mechanism is the main reason that a lot of people tend to hide their insecurities. I don't think there is anybody alive who wants to appear weak (unless they have an ulterior motive or already feel extremely confident). People try to hide their insecurities as best as they can. They equate insecurities with weakness and powerlessness. It is human nature to want to feel powerful, because in fact, we are extremely powerful beings. But unfortunately, strength and power can never be achieved from a place of guardedness. The more you hide behind your guards, the less access you have to the powers that you possess.

Most people are under the impression that one who is strong has no insecurities, but that statement could not be farther from the truth. As I mentioned before,

STEP SEVEN

there is not a person alive who is not plagued by insecurities. Instead, those we consider strong are simply not afraid, nor governed, by their insecurities. They act despite their fear of inadequacy. The strong are generally aware of their insecurities and do not pretend that they do not exist. They have embraced the fact that, sometimes, the human mind is plagued with doubt. But doubt is nothing but a reminder that you are human. If you embrace the fact that you are only human, and if anyone is going to judge you, the worst label they can give you is "human," then it might make it easier to drop the guards because we are all human and nothing more.

There is something much more important that you should consider and be aware of. As safe as it might feel to put up a guard to cover insecurities, insecurities are not the only thing that are being hidden by your guards. Unfortunately, when you hide behind a wall, you are hiding not only parts of you that you do not like but also parts of you that greatly enhance you as a person. The walls intended to protect, end up hurting you in the long run. When your walls are up, the parts of you that people see become limited to only what you are allowing yourself to show. You are basically the keeper of your qualities, and sometimes, when you hide too much, your mind also hides the good along with the bad. It does it so cleverly, that even you are not aware of what is occurring. Consider this, the things that make you most unique as an individual are the subtle traits that tend to show up when your guards are down. As much as you are a great keeper of your qualities, there are many qualities about yourself that you have yet to discover, and the best way to discover them is to let your guards down to see what is deep down waiting to surface. The freer you are, the easier they surface.

The more guarded a person becomes, the more generic they tend to be. It is extremely important for you to contemplate the idea that there is much more to you than meets the eye. There is a treasure of

STEP SEVEN

dormant potential inside of you waiting to get out, and if you tap into even the smallest portion, anyone witnessing would be impressed and in absolute awe of your uniqueness. We have access to an infinite source of intelligence, talents, skills, and abilities. It is something that we are all born with, but many of us only allow and express a very limited and restricted version of ourselves. Later in the book, I will cover this topic in more detail, but what I do want to remind you of in this step is that hiding flaws also hides your greatest potential. But you must first make the decision that it is okay to be flawed. You must make it okay for yourself to be vulnerable. And the next time you find yourself doubting yourself or your ability to decide, remember that as we navigate through life, the best experiences are in uncharted territories and the unknown.

We are constantly placed in situations that we have never faced before and that can feel scary. But if you look back at all your past experiences, you will come to realize that regardless of the situation, unless you gave up, you have always managed to find the resources to get through it all. Some challenges take longer than others to overcome, but without fail, we are always equipped with the knowledge required to rise to the occasion and make our way to the other side of each challenge.

As true as those statements may be, all of us tend to forget and get lost in the gravity of the moment. We tend to entertain the scary, and often imagined, repercussions of what can happen if we are not able to conquer the challenge at hand. We get scared because we look too far ahead and inaccurately predict the future based on fear and worry. Many of us are constantly trying to figure out how we are going to make it through a situation long before we are given the knowledge and resources required to deal with what's coming. I'd have to say that this is one of the main causes of our insecurities. We look too far ahead, unable to feel comforted, and get doubtful and insecure. We feel vulnerable and flawed. It is extremely important to remember that you are not the only person feeling this way. Everybody goes through the same thing. So, if everyone has flaws, and at one time or another feels vulnerable and insecure, why hide behind masks of security and control? Why is it necessary to appear as someone infallible and super strong? If we are all the same, can't we just admit to what we are? Can't we just be ourselves and let others do the same?

I think it is more than possible, but it takes a little bit of courage and always starts with ourselves. We must decide that we can and will release the guards that hide our flaws. We must decide to let who we are out in the open and sit there in amazement, as we realize what other wonderful qualities were also hiding behind those walls. You are not perfect, but you are very special, and you will never know how special you are until you let go of the guards. It takes some practice, and the best way to start is just making the decision to let down the guards and see them not as shields of protection but walls of confinement.

Say to yourself, "I am not perfect but that's who I am, and I don't need guards to protect me or prevent me from being my true self. It is okay to be flawed and vulnerable, and I don't care if others agree or not because I am honest with myself, and that is all that is important to me. I look forward to revealing more of my true potential. I know the moment I let down my guards, much good will come my way, not just from inside but also from those around me."

Yet I must warn you that when you become true to yourself, many people you know will start shifting out of your life. It can feel like people are dropping like flies. There is usually a moment in the interim, when people are leaving and the new people have yet to show, that feels a bit lonely. Just remember these words and endure that small window of potential loneliness of the in-between stage. You will get through it and

STEP SEVEN

what is on the other side is definitely worth the wait.

"It's not selfish to love yourself, take care of yourself, and to make your happiness a priority. It's necessary"

MANDY HALE

Step Eight:

PUT HAPPINESS ON TOP OF YOUR PRIORITY LIST

Understand that true success is happiness not wealth and status.

You can still aim to have all the things you desire, but once you understand that true success is happiness and prioritize your joy, then you will possess the ability to appreciate the present moment to a much greater extent and as a result find more moments of happiness. Everything you want to achieve is because you want to be happy, and when you come to terms with that, you can put happiness at the top of your priority list and stop waiting until you achieve your goals to be happy. Many people do not allow themselves to feel joy until they accomplish a task. It makes sense to be happy and proud of our accomplishments but if we reserve joy for those fleeting moments, we will spend the majority of our lives unhappy and unfulfilled.

Longer than I was ever called Happy, I resonated with this step so much that I made happiness my main objective in life. I knew if there was a meaning to life, it was to live in the direction of being happy. I know some people would disagree and say that it is accomplishments that give your life meaning, and although I don't completely disagree, I also know of many accomplished people who are unhappy and don't enjoy life very much. There are even examples of people in history who committed suicide even though in terms of accomplishments they were very successful. So, as I place everything into perspective, I really believe that happy people have it best. They are uplifters, and that not only benefits their own lives, but

STEP EIGHT

also makes them the biggest magnets for everyone around. Most people love and appreciate people who uplift their spirit, and people who are generally happy don't have to do much to uplift.

Just to be in some people's presence is an automatic upliftment. I know this because through some effort, I am a happiness-oriented person, and you would be surprised to see how people flock to spend time around someone happy. The one thing that needs addressing is that happy people tend to only attract people who are either happy themselves or just a step or two from happy. They repel negative people because when someone is feeling negative, to be around someone positive is very annoying. I have witnessed this on countless occasions. There are times when I just seem to get on certain people's nerves. At first, I used to take it personally, but once I learned more about people and their moods, I realized that people who are in a negative state prefer to be around people experiencing the same state, and people who are positive tend to want to be around positive people. The good news is that people who are somewhere in the middle will most likely choose to be around positive people; therefore, by being happy, you tend to attract the majority.

You might have noticed that I started using the words "happy" and "positive" interchangeably. That was no accident; being happy and having a positive outlook on life go hand in hand. Being happy takes a little bit of effort, especially in the beginning, because even though everyone wants to be happy, we have all gotten so used to not being happy that it is not usually what we gravitate toward. I understand that this step cannot be that short because it is a big topic, and most people have issues with it, but I feel that with a few clarifications, I could show you how it is that I have come to be the way that I am. If you resonate with me, you might be able to use my philosophies as a method to take a step in the direction of happiness.

Before I elaborate further, I would like to reiterate

STEP EIGHT

that the most important part of this step is simply putting happiness in its proper place, and that is at the top of your priority list. Understanding the value and the importance of happiness will allow an individual to prioritize better and look at their own life from a different perspective. Once you realize that the most important thing you can achieve is getting one step closer to happiness, then you can start to live life in a way that makes you feel more at ease with the situations that you are either in the middle of or situations that lie ahead. As you might have noticed, I did not say that the most important thing is to be happy, but instead, I said that the most important thing you can achieve is getting one STEP closer to happiness by putting happiness on the top of your list. It is nearly impossible to feel happy all the time, especially when you are in the middle of a negative situation, but at that moment, you always have a choice which way you want to direct your mood.

If you decide to dive deeper into negative situations

until they become even more powerful, you are going in the wrong direction. But if you choose to climb out and see situations from softer perspectives, ones that make them less dramatic, you will start to head in the direction of happiness. Even though you might not feel very happy at that moment, at least you are headed in the right direction. To ask anyone to feel joyful during a rough time is not very realistic. But to ask someone to hope for a positive outcome is not only reasonable, but also beneficial. Most people either view a situation with hope or fear. Once you can recognize and acknowledge the nature of your perspective, you can easily gauge if you are facing in the direction of happy (or the opposite).

So here are some key points in this step:

The first thing you must do is decide that being happy is the most important thing to achieve in life. Once you do that, you must take every possible step in achieving your happiness. This can seem impossible at

STEP EIGHT

first because so many unpleasant things happen around us that are out of our control. If you ask most people, they will say that there is too much craziness going on in their lives for them to be happy.

I think the first realization that led me to a happy state was when I understood and embodied the following statement, "it is not what you experience in life, it is how you choose to experience it." In early adulthood, I had an accidental enlightenment experience, and if I could sum up everything I learned from that experience in one phrase, it would be just that: *It is not what you experience in life, it is how you choose to experience it.* I believe that those were the greatest words of wisdom that came out of my eighteen-year-old mind. I still live by those words today.

Once upon a time, I had lost my desire to live and didn't see the point in this life because it seemed to be filled with endless drama. In my attempt to end it all, I accidentally reached an altered state of (enlightened) consciousness, and once I returned to my normal state, that phrase was all that I had brought back with me but not just the words but the true essence of what those words attempt to express. I realized that life was going to deal its blows, and unless I decided to change my perspective on all that was coming my way, I would always be in a state of uneasiness. First, not knowing what is coming, then once it comes, afraid of how unprepared I would be to handle the situation. Had it not been for that specific phrase and me doing everything I could to live up to it, this book would never even be an idea, nevertheless a reality. Today is the day you must choose to be happy, not tomorrow! That is why you should not put it off another day.

As mentioned before, most people reserve their joy for a time when they achieve a certain goal. They live in a state of unsatisfied anticipation. Once they get whatever it is they want, they get happy for a moment, and almost instantly create a new goal to accomplish, and guess what? They are once again in that interim

STEP EIGHT

where they are unsatisfied waiting for the next thing to come. It is a vicious cycle that robs people of other potentially precious happy moments. As time goes by, people only maintain their joy for a very small fraction of their life. That is a sad fate that can be avoided. That is why I believe this step can truly benefit everyone. This is a very important step and just like the other steps completely intertwined with the rest.

It is human nature to set goals and work towards achieving each one. It is normal to get happy and high for a moment, quickly get bored, and plan the next joy bringing endeavor. I don't think there's anything wrong with any of that because desire propels us forward. But what if you could stay happy between those goal-achieving moments? What if life didn't have to feel like a rollercoaster? Is that even possible? I strongly believe that it is not only possible but also extremely beneficial. Your mind is at its peak potential when it is in a state of joy giving you access to higher brain functions. Your mind also releases many beneficial hormones to maximize your potential on every level. But what I want to focus on is that as your mood dims, so does your intellect. As stress is introduced to your state of consciousness, your ability to think becomes less and less effective. So being happy not only feels good but is also extremely beneficial. You can actually say that when you are happy, you are smarter, healthier, and emotionally and physically stronger. You make better choices, and you end up in much better life situations. What could be better than that?

So now that I have told you how important being happy is, let's go over how we can become happier in everyday situations. Unless you are learning how to apply these methods in a practical way, they are of no value. The methods to reach joy are much easier than you would think. It just takes a little discipline. The most important step in reaching happiness is understanding its value. You MUST make happiness the most important goal in your life. Happiness is

STEP EIGHT

everything. Once you prioritize happiness, it is like deciding on a destination, and whether you are far or close, you can keep your attention on your desired destination. Try to face in the direction of joy at all times. What you must understand is that heading in the direction of happiness doesn't necessarily mean that you are happy all the time. It just means that you are directing yourself toward happiness, and whether fast or slow, you are headed in the right direction.

So now that hopefully you are clearer about this step, let's go to the action portion of this step. I say action, but it is mostly mental action and not physical. Now it's time to decide how you are going to view each situation of your day to make sure that you are headed toward happiness. It is action but all in your mind.

As I said earlier in this step, "it is not what you experience in life, it is how you choose to experience it." Today is the day you must start to be happy, not tomorrow; so don't put it off another day. Now is your time to decide how you want to view and live your life. Your life is such a broad time span that you must take it one situation at a time. So the best method is to just start with now. What are you going through, and how can you view that situation in a way that makes you feel better? Who are you upset with, and how can you view that person in a way that would make you feel better? Where are you in your life, and how can you view that place in a way that would make you feel better? Every step in this book is an attempt to give you a new perspective on topics that I feel need a shift in perspective. I did that to make you see those aspects of your life in a way that would make you feel happier. Now it is your turn to do it on your own regarding subjects that matter to you.

I will give you some examples, and hopefully, you will not only understand what I am trying to say but also be able to apply it on your own. First, I will show you the ideal way, and if that feels too difficult, I will show you an easy way.

STEP EIGHT

The ideal way is to take every situation and view it from a new perspective that would make you feel less bad. You must try and see the situation from as many angles as possible. This is what gives you your greatest power.

For example, if someone who cares about you starts yelling at you, instead of being mad at them, you can attempt and adopt a few different perspectives. You could say to yourself that he or she is having a bad day, and they are just taking it out on you. You could say that this is only a passing moment of your life, and in the big scheme of things, this moment is not that significant. You can scan the past and try to remember times when that person was nice to you. If all else fails, let go of the subject until you feel better enough to gain a bit more control over your perspective. Oftentimes, it is hard to change a perspective while you are upset. In those instances, you can change the subject and find something good in your life until you find yourself in a better mental state; then once you do, you can go back to the subject and change the way you are viewing the topic.

If something that has been done cannot be undone, you must decide that because there is nothing left to do, there is no point in thinking about it. If you feel bad, change the subject until you feel good enough to ponder a solution, or in some cases, cry it out with the goal of crying until there are no tears left. That is also heading in the direction of happiness.

The one problem we all have is that we try to fix something while we are still mad or upset. It is very noble to try to do that, but when the emotional part of the brain is hyperactive, your reasoning abilities diminish greatly. Oftentimes, it is much easier to change the subject long enough to calm down and feel better. Once you do, go back with the intention of looking at the topic in a way that makes you feel lighter and create a new perspective that gives the situation or person the benefit of the doubt. You will notice that

STEP EIGHT

once your mind calms down, the perspectives available tend to multiply.

If you feel that your situation is so bad that it is impossible to face the direction of happiness, and I might not know what you are going through, I will confide something about myself that I originally did not intend to include in this book. Here is a very short version of the biggest tragedy of my life! In 2014, I lost my four-year-old son and my best friend of eighteen years in a car crash. My world was shattered, and if I did not have my previous beliefs and philosophies, I don't think I would have survived. This was the worst experience of my life. I was in pieces, and I knew I had no choice but to feel every part of the pain. I had to cry and cry until the tears ran dry. Yet in every moment of sadness, I knew deep inside that I could not properly live again until I worked towards finding happiness. As I went through those heavy dark moments, I still aimed for a day that happiness would become my new reality. I can write (and will most likely write) an entire book on this chapter of my life, but for now that is all I will share so that you know there is always hope. I want you to know that even after extreme hardship, life can return to its joyful state if you prioritize your happiness. I know this for a fact because I am living proof.

I also know that sometimes it is not the big things that take away from our happiness but a combination of small things that pile up so high that they too feel like a mountain. Sometimes, those situations feel just as hopeless in the moment because life feels too overwhelming, and it's easier to look the other way and walk around with the heaviness of that pile than to attempt to chip away at it. But once you focus on your desired state of joy, you can get just enough motivation to make a very small dent in that mountain. As I mentioned before, it is not where you are now, it is the direction you are headed. A tiny movement is just as valuable as a large step. It is important to see and feel what you are capable of at this moment and do just enough not to feel overwhelmed.

STEP EIGHT

This brings me to the easy way that I mentioned earlier. If all else fails, take a nap and try again. To be honest, I just did that as I was writing this chapter. I was feeling worn down and unable to focus, so I took a thirty-minute nap. I woke up refreshed and began to chip away at this book one word at a time. I took a nap because I wanted to enjoy the process and not feel burdened by it. I had to come up with a strategy to keep working but in the direction of happiness. No one is forcing me to write this book, and it is inspired from my love for the world, but even inspired actions can feel burdensome. It is possible to lose perspective and turn something joyful into something negative. In this case, I was lucky enough to be working on this specific chapter at the right time and reminded myself that I was not faced in the right direction.

"Examine the labels you apply to yourself. Every label is a boundary or limit you will not let yourself cross."

WAYNE DYER

Step Nine:

DO NOT CATEGORIZE YOURSELF

Your potential is limitless. This falls not only in the self-image category but also in your capabilities and your self-worth.

I don't think any of us realize how much, on any given day, we categorize and limit ourselves. When I say categorize, I am talking about the little boxes we unintentionally put ourselves into. Though some don't realize they do it, all of us do it every single day when we talk about our looks, our finances, our education, our talents, our capabilities, and even our social status. We see ourselves from a very limited and comfortable view and decide to judge whom and what we are. We also judge where we are in comparison to the desired destinations in our life's journey. That view can change overtime, but it usually takes a lot of reassurance from others to make the smallest shift. But once we make that small shift, we tend to shift into a new box that is just as constricted as the last. I will give some examples to try to make it clear enough to understand.

When it comes to our looks, most people consider themselves only as attractive as they allow themselves to believe, and once they decide how attractive they "are," they see themselves as inferior or superior to others. That is the genesis of rating ourselves and others on a scale of one to ten. When it comes to dating, some see themselves as worse or better than others, and that way of thinking is extremely destructive. We don't realize how much that affects our confidence level. Your box affects how you view

STEP NINE

yourself and in turn how others view you. It is accurate to say that the way that others view you is related directly to how you view yourself. The funny part is that you don't have to consider yourself attractive for others to view you as attractive. You just need to stop yourself from feeling unattractive for others to perceive you as attractive. If you don't put yourself in a negative box, others can perceive your beauty as is.

You don't necessarily have to put yourself in an attractive box for others to see you as attractive, just don't put yourself in an unattractive box. Our insecurities often cause us to assume how others will view us long before we even meet the people that we are assuming for. We assume that because we feel inferior in some way, people that we meet will also have the same opinion. Other people don't view us from our own lens, so chances are that the things that you fixate on will not be the things others notice. The issue is that when we don't like something about ourselves, or put ourselves in a negative box, we are literally shining a spotlight on those very specific things for all to see, even if they were never going to see it in the first place. That is why categorizing ourselves in a negative way can hold us back in life and prevent us from incredible experiences.

Another example of restrictive self-categorization is when it comes to our value in the workplace. Most of us are very limited in our nature. We give our services and time a limited monetary value. We believe that we are worth a specific amount, but not more than that. I know many self-employed people who are only able to charge for their services the amount they feel comfortable asking, even though their value might be much greater. I also know many people who are only willing to ask for a certain wage for each hour that they work. If anyone reading this has ever filled out an employment application, then you know what I am talking about. Do you know that slot that asks your desired wage? Even though you might know someone making a lot more than you are willing to ask, you

STEP NINE

usually stay close to what you have been making in the past (most just add a little more but not much). We feel uncomfortable asking for more than we are used to. That is only because we have placed ourselves in a category or a box that feels familiar and oftentimes limiting.

The same goes for our education and social status. Sometimes, those two go hand in hand but not always. When people who do not have a formal education encounter people with advanced college degrees, they might feel inferior and that is only because they see the other outside of the box that they have placed themselves into. They do not feel that they have as much to offer as someone with more education, but in reality, education is not nearly as valuable as wisdom. Wisdom can be attained through infinite sources. Most gain it through life experience or even from within, long before they have experiences that traditionally add to the knowledge that I am calling wisdom. It is hard to assess, and it is best not to attempt.

A lot of these categories are placed upon us as children by our parents, and later confirmed by our friends, teachers, and school mates. It is difficult to not take others' opinions about our limitations to heart, but unfortunately, no one really knows what they are talking about and their unintended categorization of the people around them can have long-lasting negative effects. Teenagers know a lot about this based on what the other kids in school think of them, and it is easy to realize how inaccurate those assessments can be if you meet your fellow students in future reunions. Many people change, but for some, breaking out of their category is not as easy as it seems.

Unfortunately, once you categorize yourself, then you must put yourself in a box, and anything outside the realm of that box becomes unattainable by you unless you make a conscious effort to break free. As much as that box is self-created, once it is created, it

STEP NINE

does become your reality, and its effects on your life become inevitable and even harmful.

All our personal limitations come from our lack of understanding of this step. If this step was something that we fixed automatically on our own, our lives would be remarkably better. We would see improvements in many different aspects of our lives. I don't think people realize how much we hold ourselves back by the way that we view ourselves. We only feel as talented and capable as we allow ourselves to believe. We never allow ourselves to be more successful than we perceive ourselves to be, and that can cause problems. The following analogy is probably a very clear way for me to relay my understanding of this step.

Think about an eight-ounce cup and imagine filling up that cup with water from a slow dripping faucet. Once that cup is filled, however slow, it is easy to understand that the cup is not able to hold more than eight ounces of water. Now imagine dipping that same cup in an ocean, and in an instant, you can see that the cup is still only able to hold eight ounces of water and not a drop more. It doesn't matter where the water is coming from, or how fast or slow it is filled, it is the cup's capacity that determines how much water it is able to hold. Now think of yourself as that cup and the way you categorize and limit yourself as the size of that cup; then think of the abundance of the universe as that water, whether it is all around you like an ocean or whether it is coming from a specific source.

We are only able to hold as much as our self-assessed capacity, and all of us, without exception, are filled to capacity. When you look at your life, you must understand that it is you who is unable to retain further abundance, not the world withholding all that you have been wanting and waiting for. When I say abundance, I am not just speaking of monetary abundance; I am speaking about everything ranging from finance, love, friendship, joy, freedom, intellect, talent, confidence, to skill, and so much more.

STEP NINE

I couldn't stress the importance of understanding this step enough. Just the simple statement that "we are all filled to capacity" is something to be pondered deeply. There is so much depth to that statement that I felt the need to mention it again. If you just glanced at the statement and moved on quickly, then I would recommend revisiting the last paragraph until the concept properly penetrates your mind to the point of full comprehension. Only when you truly understand that you can only receive as much as you can handle, can you understand how much you are able to stunt your own personal growth by the act of self-categorization.

It's OK to reflect on the limitations and failures of the past but imperative to disconnect it from the future and its opportunities. Recognize that each experience is new, even if it feels like a replay of a previous experience. Make an effort to not assume the same outcome in a situation just because it feels familiar. There are new circumstances and players in your life, and you are not in the same place or even the same person as you were in the past, so expect a new, better, outcome in every situation because the worst thing that can happen is that you are wrong. But if you are not wrong, the possibilities are limitless.

So now I am sure you are wondering how you can stop the self-categorization that is hurting you so much. I have few statements that I feel are of much value, and once you get the gist of these techniques, I am very certain you will start to create other statements for yourself that will be just as productive as anything that I can come up with. The trick is to quickly catch yourself when you begin to self-categorize and immediately prevent self-doubt to dominate. Don't worry, you will always know when those limiting thoughts start to creep in because you will have a negative feeling in the pit of your stomach, and when you have that feeling, ask yourself as many of these questions as you'd like and try to answer as honestly as possible.

STEP NINE

1. Could I be underestimating myself?
2. Who is to say I am not better than what I give myself credit for?
3. Who made me the expert on my own potential?
4. Am I completely objective when it comes to my abilities and other aspects of myself?
5. Can I be certain what I am feeling is accurate?
6. Am I being a little harsh on myself?
7. Who is to say that I am not worth more than this?
8. Is it possible that boxes do not serve but confine me?
9. If I believe that I am only as valuable as I think I am, would it be OK if I don't limit my own value?
10. If I know that not putting myself into a box makes me limitless and filled with potential, why do I still want to put myself in a box?

Next time you find yourself judging who you are, try asking yourself these questions and see if it helps. It is not of much value just to ask yourself these questions, but it is of great value to answer these questions immediately and honestly. It is usually the answers that you give to these questions that begin the shift in your consciousness.

"Desire is the starting point of all achievement, not a hope, not a wish, but a keen pulsating desire which transcends everything."

NAPOLEON HILL

Step Ten:

KNOW THAT EVERYONE OF US IS WORTHY OF EVERYTHING WE DESIRE.

We are all put on this earth to achieve our desires and the world is in perfect balance.

I know that for every yin there is a yang and for this earth to spin so perfectly on its axis there must be balance. If the scales are off, even in the slightest bit, the equilibrium of this world ceases to exist. The reason I mention this is so I can probe into the topic of desires. I believe that when a desire is born within you, a lack is created, and the moment the lack is created, the fulfillment must be produced as well; otherwise, the universe will lose its balance. That was an idea that I came to believe at an early stage of my life, and it helped me realize that each and every one of my desires, however small, is worth being fulfilled.

I believe it is important to know that our desires are of value. When you look around and see the vastness of this universe, it is easy to feel insignificant. The undeniable truth is that compared to the size of the universe, we are extremely small. But size and value are separate things, and they must never be confused with one another.

You must first acknowledge that the desire you hold is of value before anyone or anything is able to fulfill that desire. If somehow you feel that your desire is inappropriate and not worth being fulfilled, then you must understand that you are shrinking your own vessel and blocking its ability to be filled. Many people prevent their fulfillment by trying to downplay the importance and value of the things they want. I have witnessed many people feeling guilty for wanting something that they deemed insignificant in the big picture. "There are so many people with real issues, why would anyone care if my desires are fulfilled?" "How can this desire be of any value?" "Should I even pursue this insignificant thing?" "Should I want this seemingly material thing at all?"

I was raised to believe that most desires are inappropriate and unnecessary. I am sure I am not the only one raised this way. You might be wondering what this step has to do with enhancing your inner magnet and how understanding the value of your desires could possibly enhance your charisma. This step might even seem irrelevant to some, but I am here to tell you differently. Our desires are a great part of who we are and how we prioritize our lives. They make up a great deal of who we are and not appreciating their value could potentially lead to not appreciating our own value. In order to know your own worth and appreciate yourself fully, it is important to appreciate the driving force of our personalities. Each morning, we wake up and start planning our day, then begin to figure out how to get the things that we want (whether an emotional state or a physical thing). But if you believe that your desires are important enough for the universe to fulfill, then you can appreciate its role and value.

Growing up, I was told that we can't have everything we want. We must give up on certain desires and be content with what we are given. I was taught that desire was the root of all evil and if unchecked, it can lead to destruction. I don't think that these concepts were completely wrong but learning the balance between wanting something new and appreciating what we currently have is a delicate dance worth learning. But that doesn't mean that desire in its nature is a bad or unimportant thing. We live our lives in a constant state of waiting for the next desire to be fulfilled, and if we can still appreciate what we have in the present moment, then there is nothing wrong with wanting more.

When I began my spiritual journey, I was told on countless occasions that you should not be too desirous, especially about material things. Spirituality and materialism were opposites, and in order to have one, you had to give up the other. I no longer believe that to be true. It is okay to have desires, and it is in no way, shape, or form inappropriate to want. It is the motion forward toward a desire that drives us and gives us purpose, and once we stop having desires, we stop summoning the life-giving energy that allows us to thrive. When we stop the process of wanting something new, our energies become stagnant, and the true aging process begins. That means that in order to stay young and full of energy, you must continue to explore your desires and make every attempt to fulfill them. So how could having a desire be bad when it can have so many benefits?

I am sure this is where some people will ask, "What

if those desires are harmful or destructive?" That is a valid question, and I do not disagree that some desires seem unhealthy, but it is usually not the desire itself that is unhealthy but the means one adopts in achieving it, and that is a totally separate issue altogether. We live in a world of instant gratification and that has led many people to want to fast forward to the end results. Some desires require a significant amount of time and effort, which requires patience and persistence. When desires are not fulfilled fast enough, some people take the fast and easy way out. This can show itself as dishonest actions, betrayal, and even drug use. It is usually the shortcuts people take in fulfilling the desires that can become destructive, but not necessarily the desire itself. It is of great importance to not confuse the desire itself with the means of achieving it and remember that there is always a healthy approach to achieving just about any desire.

Most importantly, this step is just about knowing that our desires are a valuable component in the

STEP TEN

creation of who we are as people. Desires help shape us, drive us, and push us forward to the next stages of our lives. They are what keep us alive and healthy. That is why you must recognize that each one of those desires is worth being fulfilled, and to stop desiring is to stop living. We are creative beings, and we exercise our creativity every time we fulfill any desire and move forward in our lives.

"One of the best guides to how to be self-loving is to give ourselves the love we are often dreaming about receiving from others."

BELL HOOKS

Step Eleven:

BE EMOTIONALLY SELF-SUFFICIENT

Know the one person whose love means the most to you is your own.

This step could have been placed as the first step because of its importance. The only way you can truly be emotionally self-sufficient is to respect, accept, and love yourself. That is why I had to cover the previous steps before I could address this one. To be emotionally self-sufficient means you no longer rely on another to sustain your well-being. It means that you stop seeking approval. It also means that when you have enough love for yourself, you do not require another to constantly reassure and validate you as a person. Having love for yourself means never having to feel codependent. All most of us try to do is find people that will shower us with love, when all this time we have forgotten that the one person whose love is readily available is ourselves. Love is the key element in emotional self-sufficiency but only when it comes from you. Yet, it is so much easier to love someone else and simply forget to give yourself the smallest compliment. The one thing I have been trying to achieve with this book is simplifying the way we love ourselves. All the previous and following steps lead to this one thing; how to love yourself more than you expect anyone else to love you. And to make it easier than before to see how special and valuable every moment of your life can be.

I mentioned earlier that this step could have been placed as the first because it is so important, but all these steps are equally important. It was hard for me to prioritize these steps, but I had no choice but to put one before the other. They are all important but being emotionally self-sufficient allows you to be more of who you are and offer more than you ever thought possible. This step puts the emphasis on understanding the value of self-love, while the other steps show you how self-love can be attained. This step goes hand in hand with every other step because at the root of every step is self-love. I believe that you must understand that it is your own love that matters most in your life before you can become emotionally self-sufficient. It is your acceptance of who you are that is of most value. But most importantly, it is knowing that the acknowledgment that your love for self is more important than anyone else's love for you that gives you the most benefit and power.

You must be able to flood your own life with love, and you must be able to achieve this without anyone else's opinion or assistance. I feel that learning how to flood your life with love is what you can achieve through all the other steps, but this step is about making the statement to yourself that the one person whose love means the most to you is your own. Knowing why you are making that statement will help you mean it and the reasons why that statement needs to be made (and meant) are endless, but I will state the most important and of course the most obvious—emotional self-sufficiency. I could not elaborate enough on its value.

Imagine a time when being rejected will not hurt as much as it used to, or a time when a relationship ends abruptly, but your life doesn't feel as if it is about to end. Imagine someone telling you that they or someone you know has a negative opinion of you but instead of falling to pieces, losing perspective, and being filled with the need to justify your "goodness," you are able to maintain your equilibrium and not take it personally. Imagine a time where you are so full of love that when someone stops giving it to you, it affects you as little as an ocean is affected when a cup of water has been taken from its volume. All these scenarios are

STEP ELEVEN

only possible when you make it your life's purpose to remind yourself that no one else's love matters as much as your own. When you remind yourself that you are worthy, special, and just as important as any other person on this planet, you are full of love. When you look in the mirror and don't pick yourself apart, you are full of love. When you make a mistake and you don't condemn or judge yourself, you are full of love. When you see a difficult path ahead yet still believe in your own ability to succeed, you are full of love. When you accept where you are in your life as a great place to be, you are full of love.

Now I must warn you, there is a fine line between self-love and arrogance. You can either believe that all are created equal and everyone is made up of the same divine spark, or you can believe that you are better than others and some are more special than the rest. I don't have to tell you which one is the healthier approach. Although seemingly the latter could be misinterpreted as truth, it is the former that is the ultimate truth.

THE CHARISMA WITHIN

Some people might be born into wealthier families, born taller, or prettier, but when you close your eyes and look inside, we are all the same. We are all made up of the same physical stuff. We are made up of atoms, molecules, cells, flesh, and bones. As much as we are all made up of the same physical stuff, most importantly, we are all made up of the same divine energy that fuels the entire world. From the smallest cells to the brightest stars in the universe, we are all made up of pure potential. It is our recognition of that which allows us to realize and access our ultimate potential and not leave it untapped. Realizing that you can accomplish anything, if you love yourself and believe in your own ability to succeed, is the magical key. It is the answer to everything.

It is ironic that self-love and belief in your own ability to succeed is what gives access to your hidden talents. Think of self-love as a magnet that draws out all your uniqueness and talents from the depths of your being. Most people have it the other way around. They

STEP ELEVEN

only start to appreciate and love themselves after they are made aware of their talents and skills. But even someone who has many obvious talents, without self-love, is still living a fraction of their pure potential. As long as you are breathing, there is more to tap into.

There is an endless well of wonders that can be accessed through self-love and appreciation, but easily denied through the act of self-loathing. There are amazing artists that have cut off their own creative flow due to their negative view or hatred of self. At the same time, there are millions of "average" people that have the potential to be extraordinary but due to their limited and negative view of self, are only allowing a mediocre version of themselves to be expressed. All individuals have a direct link to that endless well of untapped potentiality, and it is time that more begin to access and live more of their true potential. I strongly believe that learning to love oneself is one of the largest catalysts in personal revelations. You can begin loving yourself with more positive affirmations and a strict enforcement of the no self-criticism rule. When you hear that negative voice inside your head begin to criticize any aspect of you, catch yourself, and flip it around. Sometimes, it is hard to turn a negative statement into a positive, but it might be easier to just quiet your mind and change the subject. Sometimes, even that is hard to do, so that is where the next step comes in handy.

"It's the repetition of affirmations that leads to belief. And once that belief becomes a deep conviction, things begin to happen."

MUHAMMAD ALI

Step Twelve:

MAKE A DAILY STATEMENT TO YOURSELF TO BE REMINDED OF YOUR WORTHINESS.

Tell yourself that you love yourself and know that until you learn to say those words to yourself and mean it, you can never truly appreciate those words when it comes from someone else.

This step has been called positive affirmations by many authors and teachers. The first time I heard about affirmations, I thought "who actually speaks to themselves?" and I didn't quite understand the importance of this step because I never knew what good it would do to tell myself that I was valuable or worthy until I took a much closer look at the things that I was already saying to myself. I never quite realized how much I talked to myself (either in my own head or out loud). It was not the realization that I was in constant dialogue with myself that came to me as a surprise, but instead, the content of the dialogue. I am sure it comes as no surprise to you that it was mostly harsh criticism and self-doubt. If any friend criticized or doubted me half as much as I did myself, I would end the friendship in an instant. If anyone other than me pointed out my flaws as much as I did, I would kick them to the curb. After close inspection of my own inner dialogue, I realized that I had no problem tolerating my own inner critic. In fact, my inner critic was constantly berating me and making me feel inadequate. Yet, I did nothing about it.

STEP TWELVE

I began to think about how much time I spent being critical and what would happen if I began to replace those negative comments with positive ones. So, I started to play a little game. Whenever I caught myself saying something negative, I played it down, found something I liked about myself, and replaced the original statement. For example, if I felt fat, I would say, "well, I could be fatter," then find a feature that I liked about myself and remind myself of it. But realistically, I was, or still am, not able to catch myself every single time that I am being self-critical, so that is why I feel it is important to get into the habit of positive affirmations. I figure, the more time that you spend doing the things that are good for you, the less time you have for things that are counterproductive.

The best way to remember to do affirmations are either "post-it" notes on your bathroom mirror or set a reminder on your phone. I assume that we all use the bathroom multiple times a day and that is why I think leaving notes for ourselves on the bathroom mirror is always helpful. Some people might think it would be embarrassing if someone else sees that you have a note that says "you are worthy" or "you are beautiful" on your bathroom mirror. If you like, you can put symbols as reminders instead of actual notes. Feel free to get creative but do it now before you get to the next step.

Do it right now!

You can also write yourself a note, take a picture of it, and save it as your mobile phone screensaver, that way you are reminded of it every time you check your phone for calls, messages, or the time.

Here are some examples of what your notes could say:

"I am worthy of everything I desire."
"I am beautiful."
"I love myself."
"I am a divine being having a human experience."

STEP TWELVE

"I am capable of anything I put my mind to."

"I am a good person."

You can also do affirmations of things you would like to be and the things you like to achieve but make sure you are always making them in present tense because your subconscious mind does not know the difference between what you are imagining and what you are living. If you say anything in the future tense, it will always stay in the future and never enter your present moment. Your subconscious mind wants to be always right, so it is important to feed it "I am" statements that benefit you and your life. Pay close attention to what you consistently say to your subconscious mind because it goes out of its way to prove you right.

Many people have autopilot statements they make throughout the day. These statements are sometimes in their mind or sometimes out loud, but they are consistent. It is important to be aware of what automatic statements you are making to yourself on a regular basis. I know that for many years, I programmed myself to say, "I love my life." It didn't matter what was happening in my life, I would catch myself making that statement without intending to say anything at all. That was my autopilot statement.

Years later, I worked next to someone whose autopilot statement was, "I hate people." I never agreed with her but after a few years I found myself parroting those same words. I don't think I realized it until I was making that statement for quite a while. One day, I caught myself and realized that I had picked up an internal dialogue that was not my own. Another thing that I noticed was that I had slowly become less social as a person. If you knew me, you would realize how strange that sounds. I am a people person and love to be around people. Yet, the accidental adoption of someone else's statement influenced not just my thoughts but also my behavior. I must be honest; it took me a while to reprogram my mind to stop making

STEP TWELVE

that statement. The key is to be aware of what you are saying and evaluate its quality.

The point I am trying to make is that words are powerful. It doesn't matter if you say them out loud or in your mind. It is important to be aware of the things you constantly say to yourself and if they are not positive, replace them with new statements that empower you and reinforce your worthiness. Never underestimate the power of your inner dialogue because it controls your destiny. Take control, choose your statements, and repeat them on a regular basis.

"I don't tell a lie to impress you, I am what I am. It's on you to love me or hate me, I don't care."

PRAGYAN SHREE MAHAPATRA

Step Thirteen:

DECIDE NEVER TO LIE TO MAKE YOURSELF LOOK BETTER THAN YOU ARE

There is nothing wrong with who you are and where you are in your life. And either someone is going to appreciate it, or they are not, but you'd rather be surrounded by those who do.

There is one thing about a person that is more impressive than anything else in this world, and that is when a person is genuine. Everyone can tell when you are genuine, not only potential friends but also babies and animals. They read your energy and when you are genuine; they know and respect it with every fiber of their being.

I don't think I have ever heard a nicer compliment about anyone than that they are genuine. You can always tell from the tone of voice of the person offering the compliment that what they are saying is highly admirable. The word genuine is stated with great importance and value as if there is not a greater compliment than calling someone genuine. It crosses all barriers, and it doesn't matter who the person is that is being talked about, where they are from, or even their social standing; their authenticity rises above all. It puts that person in an elite category that is reserved for a limited number of people. But that "limitedness" does not have to be. There is no reason why that category could not hold more people. I not only think it is possible; I think it is where we are all headed. You

STEP THIRTEEN

can witness this when you see older people because the older people get (especially when they become much older), the higher the percentage of those who become more genuine. Most people eventually reach a time when they stop trying to be someone other than who they are, and as a result, they put all they have out there and see who is interested and who is not. But there is no reason why we couldn't reach that state at a much younger age. I feel the best way to reach that stage is to start by trying to catch ourselves in little "harmless" lies that we tell to try to look better than we are. As you can already tell, this step is very intertwined with step five, but they are not the same step. This step is about catching ourselves in little lies that don't have to be told. It is very easy for me to just say don't lie to make yourself look better and just pretend those words will penetrate the psyche and have an immediate effect. But old habits die hard and to create new habits takes a bit of effort.

I know if I were the one reading this step, the first

thing I would think is that this step is not for me because I don't think I tend to lie. But let me tell you, many people lie to make themselves look better or easily get out of a situation that would take a little more time and courage if you were to be completely honest. If you happen to be one of those people, there is nothing wrong with you. You are not alone in this and not a rare individual either. The first thing you must understand is that the lie itself is not actually rooted in deceit. It is usually your defense mechanism hard at work. So just because you conjured up a little lie to make yourself look better or take the easy way out of a situation, that doesn't make you a bad person. It only makes you human, and humans are all survivalists, and in order to survive, we have a fully functional defense mechanism that is always at work. The trick is to get the defense mechanism to work for you and not against you. The best way to do that is to learn how to soften the intensity of the system when you find it to be unnecessary. To try and shut the system down completely would not be very beneficial

STEP THIRTEEN

because the system is there to protect you, so it would be best not to try. You must understand that lying has its purpose, but once you reach a certain stage in your level of authenticity, its purpose becomes less important because your authenticity is now at stake. Of course, there are little lies that can be of value and prevent hurting another, but it is very important to evaluate the cause and necessity of those lies. Are they necessary and is there another approach you can take that doesn't chip away at your authenticity?

The key is to be able to recognize if your lie is for you to survive or if your lie has just become a ritualistic habit to look better or take the easy way out. Fortunately, you are the only one who can make that determination. I am not going to go much further into this topic because other steps delved deeper in a similar topic, but a great first step is to make the statement to yourself saying, "I will no longer lie to make myself look better or to take the easy way out of the situation." Once you acknowledge that the act of lying only diminishes your true light, it will become easier to follow through.

It is also important to consider the fact that lying requires energy, therefore, it uses up your mental bandwidth. You must remember when and what you lied about and to whom. These things take up mental resources that prevent you from being your best self. Life is hard enough as it is with our mind working at full speed. There is no need to slow it down with mental clutter.

On a final note, I would like to cover the concept that like attracts like and you get what you put out. So, if you are truthful, chances are that you will meet more honest individuals.

> "Don't judge, even if you know the whole story…[Because] the story that You know, might be completely wrong from start to end."

AKANSHA K. NATH

Step Fourteen:

DON'T JUDGE PEOPLE FROM A SINGLE ASPECT OF THEIR PERSONALITY

Try to see people as multi-faceted beings with endless aspects to their personality. Everyone has good days and bad days, so don't take a few of their aspects (or actions) and sum it up as their entire being.

Start by thinking about yourself. Think about how many aspects of you actually exist. Do you act the same

THE CHARISMA WITHIN

way when you are with a parent than when you are with a friend? Does your spouse see the same side of you as your coworkers? Do you behave the same when under pressure as opposed to when you are calm? I don't have to personally know you to know the answers to these questions, but I do know that every single person reading these questions will give me the same answer. Before you can acknowledge the fact that others are multi-faceted, you must acknowledge and observe your own multi-faceted personality.

Some people don't like to admit that they have more than one side from the fear of being considered two-faced. The truth is that even if we only had two faces, we would still be poorly equipped with the tools we need to coexist and maneuver ourselves in this world. That is why we are equipped with many aspects within the singular personality we know as ourselves. For example, many people are not very patient with their parental figures, siblings, and spouses, but they oddly tend to be very patient with their closest friends

STEP FOURTEEN

(or vice-versa).

It is wise to recognize that we all have many sides, and it is just about what side is present at this moment. Most importantly, what side of other people we bring out at each moment. As you might have noticed, it changes from moment to moment. I strongly encourage not to make anyone look like a saint and not to make anyone look like the devil. We are all everything! At the very least, we all have the potential to be everything, and there is no way that anyone can be better than what they are if they are constantly reminded of their shortcomings.

I strongly believe that we should try to see the good in people and make the effort to remind them of their positive attributes. You will be surprised to see how much gain can be achieved by everyone involved, including you. Just imagine how differently you would act if people around you focused more on your positive attributes than your negative ones. You would be inspired to be your best. The opposite is also true; if the people around you only noticed your negative qualities, it would be much harder to be your best. So, you can see the benefit of trying to seek positive aspects of the people around you and not judge them by their less favorable traits and actions. I am going to give you an example that isn't perfect but should be eye opening.

It is much easier to accept this step when observing children because most of us agree on the fact that children are still figuring out who they are, and we, as adults, usually give them the space required to make mistakes without judging their entire personality. When my four-year-old son does something wrong, he usually asks me if he is a bad boy, but the response he gets from me is, "No you are a good boy, but you just did a bad thing!" Now imagine if I called him a bad boy and equated his negative actions to who he is as a person. That would not promote better behavior and instead reinforce the idea that he is in fact, a bad boy.

STEP FOURTEEN

If his bad behavior is congruent with my interpretation of his identity, he is less likely to strive to display good boy behaviors. It is very important for me to see his behaviors just as behaviors and not who he is as a person. On that same note, if we do the same with the adults that we meet, we will not only open our minds and hearts to see different aspects of them but also inspire them to be better people.

Another important thing worth mentioning is when we judge someone based on a particular action or behavior that we do not like or understand. It is easy to get caught up in our perception of someone's behavior and jump to false conclusions. Unless you are in someone's head, you cannot truly know their motivation for any behavior. Yet, many of us use our own perspective and perception to determine another's motives. Our minds do not like ambiguity because it makes us feel unsafe. So, if there is something that is left uncertain or ambiguous, our mind will fill in the blanks with the most logical explanation based on our own personal perspective. The only problem with that is that unless we know something for certain, there is a chance (however great or small) that we are wrong. So, the best thing to do is to avoid judgment and seek clarity from a reliable source. Always remember that ASSUMPTION IS OUR WORST ENEMY.

To sum it up, people are more complex than they seem. Even those that appear to have malice intent are oftentimes victims of unfortunate life circumstances. They usually lacked something in their lives, acted out, then were labeled as someone with that behavior and later adopted it as part of their identity. All we must do is to not judge them by their unfavorable qualities and try to reflect back their positive aspects. This not only benefits us but also has a positive impact on that person's life. We might highlight an aspect of their personality that no one else has emphasized before, and as a result, become the catalyst for that person's positive change. When we judge and notice a negative

STEP FOURTEEN

aspect of someone's personality, we are only amplifying that negative quality, but when we seek the positive despite the presence of the negative, we are sending our energy to that aspect and amplifying the positive. If we do that long enough, it will have a positive effect. Even if that person does not change, they will find themselves displaying more of those positive qualities when in your presence. But who knows? Your amplification of their positive traits might have a lasting impression and reshape the personality of the people you encounter. I hope this made sense, and I have covered this topic enough for you to fully grasp the concept.

"I've learned that people will forget what you said, people will forget what you did, but people will never forget how you made them feel."

MAYA ANGELOU

Step Fifteen:

TAKE RESPONSIBILITY FOR THE ENERGY YOU ADD TO A ROOM, INTERACTION, OR CONVERSATION

Make it a point to be a positive influence in your interactions with others.

Too many of us go through life without realizing our effect on the external world, especially the people we come in contact with. We are so caught up in our day-to-day events that when we join a conversation, we rarely notice the effect of our own words or energy on the atmosphere we enter. First, let me preface that I didn't write this step for occasions when we have a positive impact on the people around us. This was intended to make us aware of times when our presence drains energy instead. Sometimes, we are in a critical mood, and by default, we begin to criticize without realizing that our words can potentially have very negative effects on the people around us. Other times, we are filled with disappointment in the people we are speaking to, completely unaware of their own personal disappointment in themselves, and end up unintentionally kicking the person while they are down.

It is human nature to have opinions about the people we encounter and especially those we are close to. It is also human nature to have negative opinions about events and actions that lead to negative repercussions. But it is imperative to read the energy in the room and see if our criticism, at that moment, is of any value whatsoever. Sometimes, our comments are not in the form of criticism but nothing more than a simple observation of a negative event (or meant as a warning). Some people are habitually living in a state of fear, warning others, or judging behaviors that are related to the topic at hand. It is easy to be that kind of person if you are genuinely concerned about a topic and care for other people's well-being but have not developed a positive approach to helping others. Regardless of the intention, it is extremely important to be conscious of the type of energy you add to the room. There is always a way to talk about a topic that lightens the mood, or at least does not make it worse than it already is.

You might have heard of the term, "energy vampires." In most cases, those energy vampires are well-intended folks wanting to express their own genuine concerns of the uncertainties and tragedies of the world, but their fear-based perspective is causing a leak in their own energy. When their energy field is combined with another's, it begins to have a negative domino effect leaving the other feeling drained. You always know if you have encountered an energy vampire because you feel less energized after your interaction. I personally do not like the term, energy vampire, because some of the biggest energy vampires I know also have the biggest hearts. They have genuine concern about the state of world affairs, but in contrast, there are many others who are just negative people that do not exhibit any warm behavior. Regardless, I feel that term is accurately descriptive, and it serves its purpose in this book.

There is not much to do about energy vampires but to recuperate after your encounter, yet it is crucial to be aware of times when you might be the one draining the energy of those around you. If we all take responsibility for the type of energy we introduce to an interaction, then there will be no concerns regarding energy vampires. It is not always easy to make sure that you are adding positivity to the room because sometimes there is nothing positive to add. But with active awareness, it is not difficult to neutralize the energy in the room and ensure that you are not

STEP FIFTEEN

enhancing the negativity. Although, if you can find a way to completely diffuse negativity and uplift those around you, then you have the ultimate secret weapon. That is the best way to become the ultimate magnet and make everyone crave your presence. The key to being that person is having the skill to either build upon an already positive conversation, swiftly change the topic from negative to positive, or diffuse the level of negativity in order to have a calming effect.

I did not originally intend to add this step to this book, but I am finishing this book in 2021, a year and a half into the coronavirus pandemic. People are divided in their opinions. The news is scary to watch. Every phone call is a potential report of yet another death in the family or friend group. There are those who believe in the severity of the pandemic and continue to be afraid, warn, and/or condemn other's nonchalant behaviors toward the virus. On an opposite note, there are people who believe that the virus is not worse than the average flu. They do not believe in vaccination and are also afraid, warn, and/or condemn other's vigilant behaviors toward the virus and how it is being handled.

Needless to say, if you are someone trying to lighten the mood, it is not as easy as it sounds. The one silver lining is that extreme times like these give us the opportunity to observe our own thoughts and actions to see how we influence the people around us. I am using the pandemic as an extreme example that is relatable at this time, but I hope this book is read long after the pandemic has left people's minds. Let me be clear, I don't mean for anyone's voice to be silenced, but I do encourage people to find a way to deliver their message in a positive way with a positive tone. Trust me, there is always a way.

My advice is to imagine the room you enter as a neutral tone or color. Then notice your impact on the room. Is the room becoming lighter and vibrant by your presence or is it becoming dimmer and duller? If

STEP FIFTEEN

you are a visual person, this is a great way to measure your influence in the room. If you are an auditory person, just be aware of the tone of voice of the people in the room and your effect on the quality of the tone.

You must be aware when you enter the conversation and then maintain your awareness as your interaction continues. When you feel, see, or hear the vibe of the room going south, see what you can say or do to soften the mood. Possibly change the subject to something lighter in nature or change your approach on how you present the problem. A great method is to put your focus on the solution and work backwards. That method has shown great results because you are coming up with solutions from a positive perspective.

I can already hear critics asking, "What if the topic is too important and needs emphasis on the potential threat?" In those cases, it is important to ensure that the ideas needing to be exchanged are addressed and covered but not longer than necessary. The problem often arises due to relentless repetition of a topic that is, at this moment, unresolvable. Sometimes, there is no solution. Other times, there are actual solutions, but the advice or warning is unsolicited. The problem with unsolicited advice is that it usually falls on deaf ears and tends to cause frustration in both parties.

Always remember that unless advice is sought out, it is often left unheard and unappreciated. Rarely does anyone want to hear an answer to a question that they never posed. Even with the best intentions, your unsolicited warning or advice can cause the energy in the room to dim. The perpetual mention of those topics is just a waste of precious moments in your life that disconnect you from your joy. Moments that will be gone forever regardless of whether you embrace fear or love. The question is, how would you like to use those fleeting yet important moments that are the building blocks of your entire life?

Conclusion

To be completely honest with you, these steps could go on and on for pages to come. But I felt that these were sufficient to get your thoughts headed toward the right direction. I know that once you are headed in that direction, new steps will come to you on their own in the form of inspiration. You will then know and be very clear on how to continue on your own. There is only one thing I am trying to achieve with my work and that is to allow you to get in touch with the real you because once that happens, you can be your own best guide, and no book will ever compare to where your inner personal insights can lead you.

You will notice that only a few of these steps were about how to treat other people. Many charisma books teach how to behave around other people and how to get others to listen to you so you can have a stronger influence on other people. Many teachers speak about making eye contact, being attentive, and giving compliments, etc. But this book was not written about the outward characteristics of what is traditionally known as charisma. It was a book focused on you becoming the best version of yourself. When you are the best version of yourself, you have nothing but your best to offer others. I hope it made sense to you why I did not focus on how to treat others and how to regulate your outward behavior.

Now, it is your job to constantly revisit and remind yourself of these steps. The more you remind yourself, the more this information seeps into your subconscious, and that is of great benefit to you. Once each concept makes its way to your subconscious and becomes a belief, you no longer need to remind yourself of any of this. You will then be on autopilot. All this information will become second nature to you

CONCLUSION

and that is when you can sit back and enjoy its rewards. So, make a daily effort to remember. You can write a note for yourself about each step and read it until you feel that you no longer need reminding. Pretty soon, you will be the one teaching these concepts to those who have noticed the change in you. I am certain that day is closer than you think.

About The Author

Happy Ali is a Los Angeles based Author and Spiritual Life Coach. His journey in helping others began in 1995 after a near death experience that caused a dramatic spiritual awakening. Happy has devoted his entire life to the exploration and study of metaphysical disciplines including the Kabbalah and the Law of Attraction. He received a B.A. degree in Psychology at the University of California, Los Angeles, and is a certified Life Coach, Health Coach, and N.L.P. Practitioner.

WWW.HAPPYINSIGHTS.NET

Made in the USA
Columbia, SC
28 March 2022